Presented to:

Date:

From:

*Volume **2**
Fortifying Your
Spiritual
Foundation*

Daily
Strength
for the
Battle ©

You,
God's Word,
5 minutes

By Scott McChrystal

Daily Strength for the Battle:
Fortifying Your Spiritual Foundation
By Scott McChrystal

Published by Warrior Spirit Publications.

Contact information:
Web site: *www.dailystrengthforthebattle.com*
E-mail: *contact@dailystrengthforthebattle.com*
Mail: *Warrior Spirit Publications*
      P.O. Box 8125, Springfield, MO 65801

Design by Marc McBride

ISBN: 978-0-615-36809-2

Printed in the United States of America
Second Printing 2011

To all military veterans, past and present, and their families who have served God and Country so nobly and selflessly. Only the Lord and those who have walked that path can fully grasp the incredible commitment, dedication, and sacrifices you have made. Thank you! The prayers and support of our nation are with you.

Contents

Growing Through Prayer:
God Answers Prayer

Learning Submission:
'What Shall I Do, Lord?'

Contents

Chaplain Scott McChrystal is a combat veteran and Spiritual Warrior who has captured the essence of winning the daily fight against mankind's' spiritual enemy. This is a good field manual for every Christian who wants to be prepared for battle."

— LTG Jerry Boykin, USA (RET)- former Commander of Delta Force and Commander of USASOC

Scott McChrystal knows God and he knows military personnel. Strength for the Battle *brings the two together in a powerful way. Scott's 30 plus years of military leadership enables him to speak with biblical authority into the minds of veterans. This is an excellent tool for bringing veterans into the transformational presence of God.*

— George O. Wood, General Superintendent, Assemblies of God General Council

Chaplain Scott McChrystal served as one of the most beloved chaplains ever at the U.S. Military Academy at West Point. This was a unique opportunity to garner experience, knowledge, and resources to produce this most inspirational devotional. Standing behind Chaplain McChrystal is a plethora of experiences in touching the lives of thousands of America's magnificent warriors. My personal experience with Chaplain McChrystal at West Point and during other opportunities verifies my confidence, for I have seen the excellence of his ministry in operation.

— Rev. Dave Roever, Decorated Vietnam veteran; military speaker

"Chaplain Scott McChrystal served as one of the most beloved chaplains ever at the U.S. Military Academy at West Point and throughout the Army. A former infantry officer and Vietnam veteran, Chaplain McChrystal's overall military service have enabled him to touch thousands of America's magnificent warriors. He will influence many more through this powerful devotional book."

— Dave Roever, decorated Vietnam veteran, Military speaker

"Every man, particularly a warrior, needs time every day with his King. Focused, purposeful, gripping time. And if he's a busy man (know any warrior who's not?), the punch of that time is served well by a directed devotional book like this one offered by my friend, Scott McChrystal, who is himself a tested warrior. And a busy, focused, and purposeful man. Enjoy the journey with him. Drive on!"

— Stu Weber, Former Special Forces Officer and Vietnam veteran, author, speaker, pastor

Therefore everyone who hears these words of mine and puts them into practice is like a wise man who built his house on the rock. The rain came down, the streams rose, and the winds blew and beat against that house; yet it did not fall, because it had its foundation on the rock. But everyone who hears these words of mine and does not put them into practice is like a foolish man who built his house on sand. The rain came down, the streams rose, and the winds blew and beat against that house, and it fell with a great crash.
(Matthew 7:24–27)

Building on the right foundation is critical in life.

Jesus teaches a powerful truth in these verses. It's a story about two builders, a wise builder and a foolish one. The wise builder built his house on rock. The foolish builder built his house on sand.

Both houses faced the same adversities — strong winds and water. The house built on rock stood. The house built on sand fell with a great crash. One house had a solid foundation. One did not.

Foundations matter. In January 2010, a devastating earthquake rocked Haiti, shattering much of the city of Port-au-Prince. About 200,000 people died. Many others were seriously injured. Damage to buildings and property was huge.

Many of the fatalities occurred as buildings and other structures collapsed. While this quake would have caused great destruction to any city, building engineers have reported that improper foundations and faulty construction unquestionably contributed to a higher death toll.

Apparently, most buildings in Haiti go up without engineers, standards, or inspections. The earthquake simply exposed the largely unregulated and haphazard construction long accepted on the island.

Metaphorically, spiritual earthquakes are rocking the lives of people today. People are struggling. Not one sector of the population, but all parts. Military service members and their families are affected like everyone else. In addition, they face the hardships that come with fighting a long war on two fronts.

Fortunately, some warriors and families are holding steady during these difficult times. Why? I believe they have built their lives on solid spiritual foundations.

Weak and strong spiritual foundations aren't always obvious on the surface. But when the storms come, the differences readily appear. Spiritually grounded people endure the adversity, and even grow stronger. Strong families not only survive; they grow closer together.

Introduction

Fortifying Your Spiritual Foundation, Volume 2 of *Daily Strength for the Battle*, provides insights from Scripture that can help you strengthen your spiritual base. The devotionals cover key areas of spiritual life and provide reliable guidance because they come directly from God's Word.

- Knowing God's Word

- Controlling Your Thoughts

- Growing Through Prayer

- Learning Submission

- Serving Others

- Knowing Your Enemy

- Growing Through Relationships

Building and maintaining a strong spiritual foundation is not easy, especially if major repairs are in order. Similar to remodeling a house, it usually takes longer, costs more, and gets messy before it's over. And there are no shortcuts.

The Scriptures promise that tough times will only get tougher. Survival will not hinge on the size of your bank account, your job title, or your reputation in the community. What matters will be your relationship with Christ and your foundation in God's Word.

Be assured of this. If you seek God through His Word, pray, and follow His ways to the best of your ability, the Lord promises you will see good results. You will mature and be effective in your Christian walk.

I pray that this devotional will be a blessing to you. ■

Christian growth and maturity take effort on a consistent basis. With consistency noted as a key principle, this book is most useful when read everyday. Reading time should take about five minutes.

Here's what you'll find in *Daily Strength for the Battle*:

• Each volume contains seven weeks of devotions, with one devotion per day.

• Each week relates to one theme.

• Each weekly theme begins with a practical illustration designed to demonstrate the relevance and importance of each theme.

• All daily devotions incorporate topics related to the weekly theme.

• All daily devotions begin with a Bible verse related to the topic.

A suggested way to approach your devotional time could include the following:

• Prayer: ask the Lord to open your heart and mind to the truth of His Word.

• Read the verse at the beginning of the devotion and then paraphrase it in your own words.

• Read the devotional.

• Try to answer the following questions:
   What biblical truth does this devotion talk about?
   How is the truth applied in the devotion?
   Do I believe this truth could be important for my own life?
   How can I apply this truth to my own life?

- Close in prayer: ask God to help you integrate this truth into your own life.

Five minutes a day may not seem like much, but you can experience wonderful growth in your Christian life and walk by consistently having these short devotions. The Lord will honor your efforts to honor Him.

Also In This Volume:

What The Bible Tells Us About God

Some people have views about God that are far removed from what God says about Himself. This section shows what God is like, in His own words as they appear in Scripture.

Some Things You Should Know About the Bible

God's Word is divinely inspired, written for all people, and meant to be read, understood, and obeyed. Read other important facts about this incredible book.

Ten Things God's Word Can Do In Your Life

God' Word teaches the path to heaven, but it also provides wisdom and guidance for living here on earth. These ten things will help you maximize the effect of God's Word in strengthening your spiritual foundation during these challenging times. ∎

Learning to Love God's Word

*Open my eyes that I may see wonderful things
in your law.
(Psalm 119:18)*

The truth of this verse can become a reality in your life. But it won't happen automatically. It must be learned.

The writer of this verse was a man who loved God and loved His Word. Although we don't know who the author was, God obviously answered the cry of this writer's heart. He learned to see wonderful things in God's Law.

Many great military men and women cannot make this claim. They desire to know the Lord in a more personal way, they want to love and revere God's Word, but they are not there yet. They live busy and useful lives serving our nation, but somehow haven't been able to tap into the pages of Scripture and see wonderful things in God's Law.

That can certainly change. It did for me. Today, I can report that the Lord has been gracious to me and opened my eyes to be able to see incredible things in His Word. I love reading and studying Scripture, and I have made it a consistent practice to do so for decades. But it is important that I shoot straight with you. It was not always this way — not even close.

The story you are about to read is true. It happens to be my story. On the surface there seems to be nothing extraordinary, nothing spectacular. But I trust it will encourage you as you search for meaning and purpose in your own life. God created us to be in relationship with Him. Getting to know Him happens in many ways, but mostly through His Word.

In 1973 I became a Christian. I was stationed with the 82nd Airborne Division located at Fort Bragg, North Carolina. My fiancée, Judy, and I were going to premarital counseling just weeks prior to our wedding date. During my first session with the pastor, he asked me, "Scott, do you know Jesus as your personal Savior?"

My honest response: "Sir, I don't have a clue about what you have just asked." The pastor explained his question and how I could accept the Lord as my personal Savior. In my thinking, I realized two things. The pastor was not going to perform the wedding unless I became a Christian. Secondly, it was time for me to make some decisions about my spiritual life. I was about to become a husband, and hopefully a father one day as well.

I told the pastor I needed a couple of days to think about it and would get back to him. I phoned him a couple of days later and told him of my decision. At the next meeting in the pastor's office, he led me in a prayer to ask God to forgive me for my sins and to invite Jesus Christ to become Savior and Lord of my life. I was 24 years old, within days of getting married to Judy, leaving the Army, and moving to another state to pursue a civilian career. Lots of change, but by far the biggest change was the conscious decision to follow Christ.

I was clueless about growing in my Christian walk. As with most military-trained people, I had learned a few things about "duty" and about "discipline." I intended to carry this training into my efforts to follow Jesus. After relocating to Kingsport, Tennessee, Judy and I began attending First Broad Street United Methodist Church. We attended the worship service on Sunday mornings. After a few months we joined a Sunday school class. We started to grow, but very slowly.

After two years in the corporate world, I reapplied to the Army and was reinstated to active duty at the very place from where we left the Army — Fort Bragg. Trust me — I was no spiritual giant, but I was determined to integrate my young faith with my service as a soldier. I carried a small Gideon New Testament in my uniform pocket and would read it from time to time.

Early in 1976 the Lord apparently decided I needed take a bigger step. Our Battalion Command Sergeant

Major had organized our first-ever unit prayer breakfast. Apparently the intended speaker had to cancel. Just a few days prior to the event, he asked me to speak. With fear and trembling, I agreed.

The night before the prayer breakfast I was still frantically searching for a topic. It seemed logical that I should use some reference from the Bible, but I was woefully ignorant. I thumbed through the pages of my Gideon Bible, hoping I would find something I recognized.

Around 2 a.m., just a few hours before I was to speak, I stumbled upon a verse I actually recognized — Luke 6:31. It was the Golden Rule. In the New International Version, it reads, "Do to others as you would have them do to you." I decided to speak from my own experiences, most of the material covering times when I didn't treat others as I should.

My memory is quite foggy about the prayer breakfast itself, but a lot of soldiers showed up. Somehow I made it through my talk that day, and amazingly what I shared seemed to resonate with the audience. I distinctly remember two outcomes of this event. First, I felt very relieved to have it over. I had never spoken publicly about the Lord before that time. Secondly, and more importantly,

I felt emboldened to share my faith with others.

We left the 82nd and Fort Bragg about 2 ½ years later and went to Fort Benning, Georgia, Home of the Infantry. While there, we found a good church and also joined a midweek Bible study. We continued to grow, Judy progressing much faster than I. Truthfully, I was still approaching my Christian growth as a duty. It wasn't fun, and I tended to look forward to the dessert we would have at the end of the study more than I did the study of God's Word. But the Lord was merciful.

In the summer of 1979, we moved to Charleston, South Carolina. I had no hint, nor did Judy, that God was about to launch me into an accelerated time of growth. It began when we started attending a little church of about 60 people. Pastor Gary preached joyful sermons, and something about the people made me think they were actually having fun in church. I started volunteering around the church, mostly custodial kinds of things. But one day Pastor Gary asked Judy and me to teach an adult Sunday school class.

We accepted, knowing full well this was well out of our comfort range. There was a licensed minister in the class, which made it even more intimidating. To our amazement, God showed His faithfulness with each passing week. We did our part in preparing; God took our efforts and turned the class into a wonderful, growing experience.

We learned from each other. All of
us learned from the Lord and His
Word.

The more I studied God's Word,
the more real my relationship with Him became.
Before even realizing it, I began to look forward
to my quiet times each morning spent studying
His Word and praying. Increasingly, I felt drawn
to read and study the Bible.

On a Sunday night in January 1980, I had an
experience that was to change the direction of
my life. Following a sermon that Pastor Gary
preached, I went down to the altar to pray. As I
was praying, I sensed the Lord was speaking to
my heart, telling me I was supposed to go into full-time
ministry. I left the altar, quite stunned by what I thought I
had heard from God. I said nothing to Judy about this.

Several weeks later, I dared to tell Judy that I thought
God might be calling me to full-time ministry. She didn't
faint, but was definitely surprised. We agreed to pray
and seek God for confirmation. Since I had a 3-year
commitment to the Army for graduation education, we
didn't need to do anything quickly.

The one step I did take was to begin working
toward a preaching license. I signed up for the required
correspondence courses, all focused around reading and

learning the Bible. For the next year, I spent extensive time almost every day reading God's Word.

A year later, I learned that I could only become a military chaplain on active duty if I did so as a Captain. The choice was clear. Do I continue as an Infantry officer, or did the Lord want me to resign my commission, go to seminary, and reapply to come back in as a chaplain?

The rest is history. The Lord opened the door for me to serve as an Army chaplain for more than two decades.

Looking back, I fully believe God would have honored my choice to remain as an Infantry officer versus pursuing the military chaplaincy. What was important was not the career I chose, but rather the decision to make my relationship with God my top priority. Central to that decision was to make God's Word my priority.

Like a lensatic compass used for land navigation, God's Word is a sure guide for life. The Lord has created you for His pleasure and purpose. He certainly doesn't want you guessing as to which direction to go.

On the authority of God's Word, I firmly believe that you can become like this Psalmist. You can delight in God's Word and find many wonderful things that will enhance your relationship with God and provide the guidance and assurance that you are spending your life doing what He has planned. ■

Taking Inventory

And this is the testimony: God has given us eternal life, and this life is in his Son. He who has the Son has life; he who does not have the Son of God does not have life.
(1 John 5:11,12)

Good leaders know that communicating truth is extremely important if your followers are to trust you. Shooting straight with them is definitely the way to go.

Our Heavenly Commander knows this and has chosen to communicate truth through His Word. In these verses, the apostle John testifies that God has made a way for every person to have eternal life through His Son, Jesus Christ. But John doesn't stop there. He plainly states that those who have Christ have eternal life. Those who do not have Christ do not have eternal life. There is no middle ground.

In the midst of busy lives, it's tempting to think only about the here and now. But Jesus spoke many times about the afterlife and the importance of preparing for it.

The Lord is not speaking in riddles. Isn't it time for some honest assessment? Have you committed your life to Christ?

Jesus wants you on His team. ■

Friend or Enemy?

But solid food is for the mature, who by constant use have trained themselves to distinguish good from evil.
(Hebrews 5:14)

Counterinsurgency operations (COIN) can be deceptively hazardous. Often the most difficult task is identifying the enemy from among the local populace. In many cases friend and enemy look identical. To confuse matters further, the enemy strives to convince the people that the insurgents have the people's interests at heart.

In Afghanistan, our military leadership has identified the enemy's strategy and is pursuing effective measures to separate insurgents from the population.

As soldiers in God's army, we face an enemy who excels in COIN. His tactics focus largely on preventing Christians from discerning good from evil.

Looking around at our culture today, you see much that does not match the lifestyle or behavior that God wants us to practice. Sadly, many Christians don't know the difference.

As soldiers in God's army, are we defenseless? Absolutely not! We simply need to read the Book.

Don't let the devil pull his tricks on you. Get trained with God's Word! ∎

Planning Ahead

Therefore the Lord himself will give you a sign: The virgin will be with child and will give birth to a son, and will call him Immanuel.
(Isaiah 7:14)

As Commander in Chief of the universe, God has repeatedly proven He is a long-range planner, and a very precise one.

About 700 years before Jesus Christ came into the world, God used a prophet named Isaiah to announce that God's Son would be born of a virgin. It happened.

"Impossible!" you say? No — supernatural to us, but easy for the Lord. Remember — He spoke the world into existence.

Here's a thought: If God is such an awesome planner, doesn't it make sense to follow His plan for your life?

Taking this to a personal level, do you believe that our Lord created you unique from anyone on the planet? Part of the package is that He has designed your life with a special plan and purpose.

Perhaps you think it's too late to get in synch with God's plan for your life. Too much has gone wrong.

This is absolutely not the case. Don't try to chart your own course. God stands ready and able to help you — now. ■

With Us Always

*Therefore go and make disciples of all nations,
baptizing them in the name of the Father and of
the Son and of the Holy Spirit, and teaching them
to obey everything I have commanded you. And
surely I am with you always, to the
very end of the age.
(Matthew 28:19,20)*

Professional soldiers understand the need to obey
orders. Unless the orders are illegal or immoral,
soldiers are expected to carry them out to the best of
their ability.

It's standard operating procedure for commanders
to issue the mission statement with a few specifics,
but not all of them. They usually leave the "how" to
their subordinates to figure out. Bottom line, however:
Commanders expect followers to complete the mission.

For the Christian soldier, these verses comprise one
of the most important and clearly expressed orders
Jesus Christ ever issued. Notice that the Captain of our
Salvation doesn't micromanage "how" each soldier
carries out His guidance. He leaves the details to us.

But make no mistake. He expects every soldier in His
army to participate.

This is a tall order. But remember, you're not in this
alone. Jesus Christ will be with you — ALWAYS. ∎

Claim His Promises

Then Caleb silenced the people before Moses and said, "We should go up and take possession of the land, for we can certainly do it."
(Numbers 13:30)

This excerpt relates to one of history's earliest recorded deep reconnaissance missions. Of the twelve patrol members sent by Moses to spy out the land that God had promised to give the Israelites, only Joshua and Caleb really believed it would happen.

It's notable that the people also chose to believe the faithless report of the ten spies. Sharp debate arose within the Israelite camp, and at one point unbelief threatened to cancel plans to cross the Jordan and inherit the Promised Land.

Fortunately, there were two men who still believed God, Joshua and Caleb. These words by Caleb represent his confidence in God's ability to make good on His promises.

Many soldiers in God's army could accomplish much more in life if they would follow Caleb's example. Instead of looking at the obstacles, Caleb looked to God's promise and His ability to deliver.

Do you believe God can make good on His promises in your life? Claim His promises and exercise your faith. God will not let you down. ∎

Successful Plans

Commit to the Lord whatever you do, and your plans will succeed.
(Proverbs 16:3)

In military operations, a course of action (COA) is simply a plan of action. Normally, the staff develops two or three COAs for the commander's consideration. Together they select the plan that is most likely to succeed.

Staff members go to painstaking effort as they perform detailed analysis in developing each COA.

But what happens once these COAs have been developed? Do the staff members merely decide among themselves which course of action to pursue? No! The staff continuously receives guidance from the commander before one COA is selected as the plan to execute.

It's the Lord's intent for us to work together with Him as we make plans in our own lives. It's not a one-sided venture. We do our part. God does His part. Trouble happens when we step out on our own. Our Heavenly Commander does not want us to operate without His guidance.

As you plan COAs for your life, are you consulting your Heavenly Commander? Do you have His guidance and approval? If you do, this verse says you will succeed! ∎

Grow Up!

Like newborn babies, crave pure spiritual milk, so that by it you may grow up in your salvation.
(1 Peter 2:2)

The United States Navy Sea, Air and Land Forces, commonly known as the U.S. Navy SEALs, are the Special Operations Forces of the U.S. Navy. Anyone can volunteer, enlisted or officer. Training is incredibly tough and demanding.

Regardless of age or ability, every "recruit" in SEAL training must grow — physically, mentally and emotionally. Those who don't grow leave the program. Why? SEAL missions are tough. Only those who have grown will survive and be able to contribute to mission accomplishment.

The Christian life is similar. Training is tough, and there are no shortcuts. The enemy of our souls is a formidable foe. Those who don't grow in Christian maturity greatly limit their effectiveness. Unfortunately, many Christians remain like spiritual babies and never grow into spiritual warriors.

Tired of not growing? Is life beating you up? Decide today to seek God with all of your heart. Read your Bible and pray with an earnest desire to know God better. He will honor your efforts. You will grow.

God's Word says you are more than a conqueror! ■

Not a Spirit of Fear

For God hath not given us the spirit of fear; but of power, and of love, and of a sound mind.
(2 Timothy 1:7, KJV)

Control over our thoughts can have profound consequences in life, especially as it relates to our relationships — with God and with people.

One of the most challenging areas within our thought life pertains to how we deal with fear. Far too many people spend their lives in bondage to fear. Let me cite a few examples.

- Won't fly in an airplane

- Won't use elevators

- Won't drive a car

- Won't consult a doctor, even though they're very sick

- Won't get out of a rut because they're afraid of failure

- Won't be themselves

- Won't exercise or be active

- Won't go near water — can't swim

Before going further, know it is normal to have fears. I may not have the same fears you have, but we all have them. Some of our fears are very private, known only to God and ourselves.

That said, the Lord doesn't
want us to remain in bondage
to our fears. In fact, Scripture
contains hundreds of times when
God exhorts us not to be afraid.
The verse shown above is just one example. The
apostle Paul is writing to encourage a young
pastor named Timothy to use his God-given
talents in his ministry and not to let fear stop
him from fulfilling God's purposes.

Notice the first part of the verse: "For God
hath not given us the spirit of fear." Paul goes
on to say to Timothy, "But of power, and of
love, and of a sound mind."

So how do we deal with our fears? I believe
it starts by accurately identifying the fear and
admitting that it is a problem.

Second, it is essential to apply the truth of this verse
to the situation. The Lord doesn't want us to live with
a spirit of fear. We must believe this truth. A good step
may be to pray to God and ask Him to remove the fear
or give us the strength and courage to overcome the fear.

Often the third step is an action step. How is the Lord
leading you? Frequently, trusting God for answered
prayer means we step out in obedience to whatever we
believe the Lord wants us to do.

I find it fascinating that God can use anything He
chooses to help people overcome their fears. Often it's

another person. Let me cite two examples from my experiences in Vietnam.

I recall a young Specialist in my first infantry platoon. He had less than a week remaining on his tour at the time I joined the platoon. After a day or so at our field location, I noticed that this soldier never left his foxhole. I am not sure he left even to relieve himself.

I mentioned this to my platoon sergeant, an experienced combat veteran. He told me that it was not unusual for soldiers getting near the end of their tour to start becoming more cautious, and even fearful. The fear of being wounded or killed at the end of a combat tour caused some to grow extremely timid.

Most of the time fellow soldiers understood this and made allowances. Sometimes, however, leaders permitted this to go on entirely too much and created morale issues within the unit by choosing not to confront the behavior.

Being new to Vietnam, I took the advice of my platoon sergeant and chose not to intervene. Within a week the soldier was on his way back to the United States. But I did file this incident in my mind for later reference.

Example number two is similar, but not in the outcome. Fast-forward 10 months. I was an infantry platoon leader in another unit. This time, I was the person with the most time in country.

Our battalion was very close to being inactivated and sent back to the U.S. However, we still had a few more weeks of field time remaining. Missions included interdicting enemy supply lines. Search and destroy is a more direct way to describe what we did.

My platoon was operating from a jump firebase. We would send roving patrols during the day and usually deploy one stationary ambush patrol during the hours of darkness. We rotated ambush duty among the squads, with the squad leader designating the individuals who would participate in the ambush. Usually, one or two squad members would remain behind at the firebase.

I began noticing that squad leaders were leaving the same people back each time. Truthfully, they left their less reliable soldiers. If a firefight broke out, they wanted their best men with them. In one sense I could understand that.

But it still bothered me that the same soldiers were being left behind while the others took all the risks. Additionally, the soldiers being left behind were losing confidence in their own capabilities to pull their share of the load.

Finally I had had enough. These soldiers were going on an ambush patrol, and I was going to lead it. The platoon sergeant and squad leaders thought I was nuts, but went along with the plan.

We spent the day selecting the ambush site and making preparations. Next we rehearsed actions in the event of enemy contact. As daylight rapidly disappeared, we left our secure location and walked to the ambush site. We organized the ambush location, positioning each man in place as we had done in rehearsals.

No one slept. No one talked. We simply watched and listened. It was a long night. The biggest challenge, frankly, turned out to be the mosquitoes.

Finally, the first signs of daylight appeared. Soon our ambush patrol was completed and we walked back to the firebase. As we reentered the wire, I noticed that each member of the patrol seemed to walk a little more upright and with more bounce in his step.

It was obvious that every man in that patrol felt good about what had happened the previous night. Going on the ambush had done much to reduce fear. Taking those soldiers on ambush patrol that night was the right thing to do.

Fear can be a crippling emotion, and it can occur virtually anywhere, anytime. But we don't have to be helpless victims. The Lord will help us.

Do you have a nagging or even crippling fear in your life? I encourage you to identify it, seek God's help, and take action to overcome it. ■

Overcoming Anxiety

When anxiety was great within me, your
consolation brought joy to my soul.
(Psalm 94:19)

The competitive climate of the military is a constant source of anxiety for many military members and families. The concerns are real. Job security, promotion opportunities, and retirement planning are only a few of the critical areas affected.

The War on Terrorism has created additional sources of anxiety. Not only is there the stress of surviving combat, but there are the additional challenges of frequent deployments. Military families must face the strains associated with preparing for deployment, the deployment itself, and the challenge of reintegration following deployment. This can create a great deal of stress for the entire family.

Perhaps you are experiencing anxiety. The Psalmist's message is one of hope. When he felt anxious, God's comfort brought joy to his soul. God's Word brings perspective on life's challenges because it helps us realize that the Lord is greater than any problem.

Scripture emphasizes that God is no respector of persons. If God brought comfort to the Psalmist, He will do it for you.

Take heart. Don't let anxiety get the best of you. Let God's comfort be a source of joy to your soul! ■

Controlling Your Thoughts

Bottom-Line Assurance

Who shall separate us from the love of Christ?
Shall trouble or hardship or persecution or famine
or nakedness or danger or sword?
(Romans 8:35)

Military life can be hard — very hard. At times the sacrifices demanded of soldiers and family members can seem unbearable: long hours, harsh conditions, separation, loneliness, frequent moving, and even life-threatening danger.

The protracted nature of the War on Terrorism continues to test our military community to the limit. PTSD, divorce, and alcohol are only a few of the problems. Increasingly, we are seeing the toll on the children of military families as well.

Perhaps you've thought, "Where is God in all of this?" If you have, take heart in knowing that many others have felt the same way.

God has good news for you. The answer to the question the apostle Paul poses in this verse provides the bottom-line assurance we all need.

God hasn't gone anywhere. He's here. Nothing can separate us from the love of God which is in Christ Jesus our Lord.

NOTHING! ■

Never Deserted

*At my first defense, no one came to my support,
but everyone deserted me. May it not be held
against them. But the Lord stood at my side
and gave me strength, so that through me the
message might be fully proclaimed and all the
Gentiles might hear it.
(2 Timothy 4:16,17)*

History has demonstrated repeatedly that even
military leaders with great physical courage can
struggle less successfully on the moral and ethical
battlefield.

One reason that makes moral/ethical decision-
making so hard is the aloneness factor. This occurs
when those around you remove their support and leave
you to stand alone. It's not a fun place to be.

The apostle Paul felt this way in his defense of the
gospel. He discovered, however, that he wasn't alone
after all. As he reports in his writing to Timothy, the
Lord stood by his side.

The aloneness Paul experienced is something we will
all taste at one time or another. But we will never be
truly alone.

Perhaps you are facing a tough decision in your own
life and are standing with little or no support from
others. Take heart. Maintain your stand. The Lord is
standing with you. He is on your side. ∎

Think on These Things

Finally, brothers, whatever is true, whatever is noble, whatever is right, whatever is pure, whatever is lovely, whatever is admirable — if anything is excellent or praiseworthy — think about such things.
(Philippians 4:8)

The U.S. military has the mission of winning this nation's wars. All branches of our military need warriors who are winners in life.

Integral to being a winner is maintaining a positive, winning attitude. This means we have to control what we think about.

So how do we maintain control over our thoughts and keep a winning attitude? The Lords exhorts us to think about things that are true, noble, lovely, admirable, and so forth.

Keeping a healthy mind and positive attitude is much like maintaining a strong body. There are many choices in the foods we eat. If we eat foods that are high in calories, high in fat, and low in food value, our bodies will suffer. It works the same with our minds.

So, warrior, what kinds of things occupy your mind? Are they true, noble, admirable? If not, toss the bad stuff and start thinking good stuff.

Isn't it about time that you took charge of your thoughts? ∎

Delight in God's Law

Blessed is the man who does not walk in the counsel of the wicked or stand in the way of sinners or sit in the seat of mockers. But his delight is in the law of the Lord, and on his law he meditates day and night.
(Psalm 1:1,2)

Truth is key, both at the personal and national level.

Consider the fact that the U.S. has been engaged in a protracted war against terrorism. Our leaders have rightfully determined that successful counterinsurgency tactics necessitate winning the hearts and minds of the people in Iraq and Afghanistan. We must successfully communicate truth about our nation's motivations and intent. If we can't do this, we fail.

The Christian life likewise hinges on hearing and believing the truth. Fortunately, we have a reliable source for truth — the Bible.

Notice the Psalmist's counsel in these two verses. Don't walk with wicked people, don't stand with sinners, and don't sit with mockers. You won't find truth in any of these places.

Do delight in God's Word. It's the truth. Meditating on it will transform your life.

You have a choice. Whose report will you choose to believe? ∎

Meditate on God's Wonderful Works

They will speak of the glorious splendor of your majesty, and I will meditate on your wonderful works.
(Psalm 145:5)

David was a warrior. He killed Goliath. He led Israel to many victories over surrounding nations. But, bluntly stated, he had a lot of blood on his hands.

How did he cope? How did David avoid becoming crippled by post traumatic stress?

David's writings give us a clue. He devoted much effort to praising God and meditating on the Lord's wonderful works. Doubtlessly, he spent time studying and reflecting on God's marvelous creation — the earth, the heavens, the stars, and the people God had made for himself. In another psalm David wrote, "I praise you because I am fearfully and wonderfully made" (Psalm 139:14).

Bottom line: David took control of his thoughts. Instead of fixating his mind on the lowly and the base things of life, he chose to meditate on the awesome things God has done. Read all of Psalm 145. Read other psalms David wrote — about 75 in all. God's works are amazing!

David constantly occupied his mind with good and wholesome thoughts — God's incredible works.

Try it! You'll notice the difference in your own life. ■

Take Every Thought Captive

*We demolish arguments and every pretension that
sets itself up against the knowledge of God, and
we take captive every thought to
make it obedient to Christ.
(2 Corinthians 10:5)*

Controlling our thoughts is not for the weak or faint-hearted. It takes intentionality and determination.

True, we can't prevent every negative or evil thought from entering our minds. In our culture today, we are constantly bombarded by ungodly, unwholesome words and images.

But the apostle Paul says we are not helpless. We have to take the offensive. As arguments and pretensions that oppose God enter our minds, we are told to demolish these arguments.

How? We are to take captive every thought and make it obedient to Christ.

Will this work? Absolutely! But it takes consistent effort. It also requires that we be alert to identify false and evil thoughts and rid them from our minds. A half-hearted effort will not work. Like a good surgeon going after cancer, we must remove all of it.

An important point: We cannot do this in our own strength. It's a spiritual battle. But in the power of the Spirit, we can take every thought captive to Christ. ■

God Answers Prayer

> *This is the confidence we have in approaching God: that if we ask anything according to his will, he hears us. And if we know that he hears us — whatever we ask — we know that we have what we asked of him.*
> *(1 John 5:14,15)*

It was a cold, overcast day in Tuzla, Bosnia, in March of 1996. The biting wind made it even more miserable. As the Task Force Eagle Chaplain, I was visiting the Aviation Brigade unit ministry teams located at Comanche Base Camp. Having just arrived, I was talking with the Brigade Chaplain and one of the Battalion Chaplains, Chaplain (CPT) Dan Wackerhagen.

Suddenly, the base camp emergency alarm sounded and a soldier came running by us saying that some of our soldiers had been injured. Immediately the three of us began walking quickly to the scene of the accident. It was a long walk because the airfield was nearly a half-mile long. When we arrived we found that a huge machine-gun tower constructed out of 20-foot-long, 12-inch-square beams had collapsed and fallen on some soldiers.

Given the limited medical resources available, we were experiencing a mass casualty event. There was yelling and screaming as soldiers rushed to the scene. It was a terrifying sight.

One of the soldiers was pinned to the ground by a huge beam. The beam had fallen horizontally across the small of his back. The beam was too large to pick up. The engineers quickly brought shovels and began to dig under him until they could slide him out from under the beam.

A sense of dread had fallen over those present because of the potential seriousness of the soldier's injuries. It was one those things that makes one queasy to look at. The victim was sobbing and moving his arms, but his legs were completely limp. He kept repeating, "I can't feel my legs!"

Soon the engineers slid a 12-foot-long, 2 x 10 board under him and pulled him out from under the beam.

The medical evacuation team had just arrived and was making its assessment. The soldier was not a pretty sight. In addition to coughing up blood, he was bleeding heavily from the upper skull area, nose, and left ear. The likelihood of multiple fractures and internal bleeding in the chest cavity seemed high. Paralysis in one or more limbs was certainly possible.

The medics tried to be as gentle as they could, but the process still appeared brutal. In life and death situations, medics cannot afford to allow pain to slow their work. The soldier was in obvious agony, screaming the entire time, and even louder as they examined his injuries and started an intravenous injection to keep him from going into shock.

For those not accustomed to emergency first aid, it was unsettling to say the least. I turned and watched numerous soldiers grimace as they listened to the screams. Most chose to walk away. With the other trauma surrounding the accident, it was more than they could endure.

The medics now strapped him down to the board to ensure that his neck and back could not move. They then carried him to the chopper that was standing by and loaded him aboard. But there was a problem.

The board to which they had strapped the soldier was extending out both sides of the helicopter. It was not a safe situation. They placed the injured soldier back on the ground. One of the engineers produced a hand crosscut saw and proceeded to saw off both ends of the board.

Every time the engineer cut a stroke, the injured soldier cried out in pain. It seemed like it was taking forever to get him out of there. It was excruciating to watch. The medics, pilots and engineers surrounding him were unnerved and arguing about what to do.

But, then, God intervened in a special way. Chaplain Wackerhagen stepped near the soldier. He knelt down and laid his hands on the injured soldier's head and began to loudly recite the Lord's Prayer. Something very special happened. Everyone there seemed to sense God's presence. The soldier calmed down and became very quiet, peaceful and still.

The engineer cutting the board began to make faster progress. Every soldier there was reciting the Lord's Prayer along with Chaplain Wackerhagen. He finished the prayer, and they got the soldier on the chopper and to the hospital.

After remaining at Comanche Base Camp for a couple more hours, I returned to headquarters at Tuzla. As much as I tried, I could not get the injured soldier off my mind, particularly the images of him screaming in pain as the medics tried to help him.

The next day the brigade chaplain called with amazing news. The injured soldier was doing fine. The doctors had made a thorough examination and determined that the extent of his injuries were a few minor bruises. He was released from the hospital and returned to his unit.

I believe God did a miracle at Comanche Base Camp that day because a military chaplain turned to God in prayer. With him, a bunch of cold, dirty, tired, and worn-out soldiers called upon His Name in time of crisis.

The lesson is simple, but profound. No matter how out of control things seem to get on the ground, always remember to pray. God will help you. ■

He Will Provide

*Ask and it will be given to you; seek and you will
find; knock and the door will be opened to you.
(Matthew 7:7)*

Combat Service Support (CSS) is a critical Battle Operating
System in modern warfare. As the military trains to respond
to any crisis around the globe, it is imperative that military
leaders understand CSS in order to deploy, fight, and win.

In short, CSS is about commanders and units having what
they need to accomplish the mission in times of peace and of
war. This is critical as units prepare for combat. It becomes
even more crucial in conflict and sometimes very difficult to
achieve.

Worst case, sometimes it's just not possible. When this
occurs, we run the risk of losing the fight.

Spiritual warfare is tough, but there is good news. Our
Heavenly Commander runs the most efficient CSS in this
universe. One of His names is Jehovah Jireh, meaning "the
Lord provides." And one more important point — God's
ability to provide never falls short. Never.

How does God's provision work? It works very simply.
Through prayer, tell the Lord about your needs. He will
provide! ■

*P.S. And don't think that any request is too trivial or
unimportant for God. He cares about you!*

I Have Heard Your Prayer

> *Then Isaiah son of Amoz sent a message to Hezekiah: "This is what the Lord, the God of Israel, says: I have heard your prayer concerning Sennacherib king of Assyria."*
> *(2 Kings 19:20)*

Around 700 B.C., a desperate king named Hezekiah prayed. His tiny nation of Judah was about to be overrun by the armies of Sennacherib, ruler of Assyria. No odds maker in Las Vegas would have given Judah the remotest chance of surviving.

But Hezekiah prayed. The Lord heard Hezekiah's prayer and sent the prophet Isaiah to deliver the answer. "I have heard your prayer concerning Sennacherib." He went on to say that the Assyrian army would not shoot a single arrow before they would be chased back to where they had came from.

That night, an angel of the Lord killed 185,000 Assyrian soldiers in their own camp. The next morning, the remainder of the Assyrian army executed a hasty retreat back home.

The army of Judah didn't have to lift a finger. The Lord had won the battle for Judah.

We all face our own battles, and many exceed our own capabilities to handle. Like Hezekiah, we can pray. ■

I Am a Person of Prayer

In return for my friendship they accuse me, but I am a man of prayer.
(Psalm 109:4)

David needed God's help — again. Ever felt that way?

As Psalm 109 opens, we immediately find that he is in trouble. Wicked and deceitful men have spoken lies and deceit about him. They have attacked him with words. In exchange for his friendship, they have thrown accusations.

We know David was a shepherd, a warrior, a poet, and a king. Now, by his own description of himself as he talks to God, we learn he is a man of prayer.

David is in a tough spot for sure. But then he says, "But I am a man of prayer."

Is David bragging here? Is he acting like some holy roller who thinks he is better than anyone else? No, he's not. This man, who killed the 9-foot giant Goliath, is in another fight. This time against vicious and wicked men.

He knows he can't handle this kind of trouble in his own strength.

He calls upon God. He prays.

What about you, especially when trouble comes your way? Are you a man or woman of prayer? ∎

I Will Listen to You

*Then you will call upon me and come and pray to
me, and I will listen to you. You will seek me and
find me when you seek me with all your heart.*
(Jeremiah 29:12,13)

It was not a good time for Judah. Many of her
citizens were living in exile in Babylon. The capital city,
Jerusalem, would fall in the near future. Among the
Jewish people, hope was scarce.

But God wasn't finished with this tiny nation. He
commissioned the prophet Jeremiah to proclaim a
message of hope and comfort. The Lord told the exiles
that their captivity would not last forever. In 70 years
He would bring them home.

He also told the discouraged captives that He
welcomed their communication and would both hear
and answer their cries.

But God stated that there would be one condition:
that they must seek Him with all of their heart. In
other words, the Lord insisted that they pray with
sincerity.

Have you ever thought about all of the hang-ups we
humans have about God and prayer? We make it so
complicated!

God doesn't. God simply tells us to seek Him like we
mean it — with all of our heart. ■

Don't Keep Babbling

And when you pray, do not keep on babbling like pagans, for they think they will be heard because of their many words.
(Matthew 6:7)

Few subjects generate more guilt than the subject of prayer. We talk a lot about prayer. And yet, when all is said and done about prayer, more is said than done.

Sure, prayer is a powerful spiritual weapon. Satan will employ any tactic necessary to prevent us from communicating with our Heavenly Father through prayer.

But this guilt thing — does God want us to feel constantly condemned because we don't pray enough?

In His Sermon on the Mount, Jesus talks about prayer. He specifically tells His listeners that long, rambling prayers designed to look spiritual or impress others just don't cut it.

Should we be men and women of prayer? Absolutely. But perhaps some of our guilt is false due to wrong expectations regarding how much time we should devote to prayer.

Our Lord understands busyness, obligations and schedules. Jesus had a life filled with demands. So whether we pray for 1 minute, 5 minutes or 60 minutes, rest assured that He recognizes and rewards prayer that comes from the heart. ∎

Divine Perspective

When I tried to understand all this, it was oppressive to me till I entered the sanctuary of God; then I understood their final destiny.
(Psalm 73:16,17)

Can you remember losing your perspective about a situation? It could have involved almost any topic — relationship, job, health, money, or disappointment.

Although we often tend to associate prayer with asking God to change something, sometimes He simply chooses to change us. Consider Asaph, the writer of Psalm 73. Asaph was reflecting on a time when he nearly lost his spiritual footing.

Why? He clearly tells us that it was because he envied the arrogant and wicked people around him. These people were filthy rich and seemed to be living carefree lives. They lived only for themselves and paid no attention to God whatsoever.

Asaph questioned whether his attempts to serve God were worth the effort. But one day he went to the temple, gathering with other worshippers, and talked to the Lord about this. God showed him that these people might be enjoying themselves temporarily here on earth, but their final destiny would be destruction.

Now Asaph understood. Through prayer, God had given him perspective. The Lord will do the same for you. ∎

Powerful Prayer

*The prayer of a righteous man is powerful and
effective. Elijah was a man just like us. He prayed
earnestly that it would not rain, and it did not rain
on the land for three and a half years.
(James 5:16,17)*

Prayer is a powerful spiritual weapon, especially
when the person praying is trying to live righteously.

James, the writer of these verses, references one such
righteous man — Elijah. Elijah was a prophet of God.
At one point, the Lord decided to punish Israel and
King Ahab for their sinful ways, especially idolatry.
The punishment — drought and famine. Elijah prayed
and it did not rain for 3 ½ years.

I recall visiting with a 5-year-old boy in a hospital in
Richmond, Virginia. I gathered with him and his family
the evening prior to the boy's scheduled heart surgery.
He had a large hole in his heart needing immediate
repair.

As I was about to pray, the boy asked if he could
pray. Of course I said yes. His words were few: "Lord,
I pray I survive. Amen."

No surgery ever happened. God healed his heart
supernaturally. The prayer of this righteous young man
was powerful and effective. ■

'What Shall I Do, Lord?'

*"What shall I do, Lord?" I asked.
"Get up," the Lord said, "and go into Damascus.
There you will be told all that you have been
assigned to do."
(Acts 22:10)*

The speaker is Saul. He's talking to God and he's not blowing smoke with the question. He earnestly desires an answer and is ready to execute whatever God tells him to do. He's finally ready to submit.

Were he alive today and serving in the military, Saul would likely be a flag officer. He possessed a multitude of the qualities sought after in a leader within our Armed Forces. No one was more mission-focused.

For a long time, however, submission was not on Saul's radar. Let me tell you the story surrounding Saul's decision to submit to God's will. It has application for us today.

In the days following Jesus' crucifixion and resurrection, the Early Church began to grow in Jerusalem. There was much opposition, however, primarily led by the Jewish religious leaders. They wanted to stamp out Christianity before it could get a foothold, and they went to extreme lengths to accomplish this. One of their young leaders was a man named Saul. Consider Saul's own words describing himself:

I am a Jew, born in Tarsus of Cilicia, but brought up in this city. Under Gamaliel I was thoroughly trained in the law of our fathers and was just as zealous for God as any of you are today. I persecuted the followers of this Way to their death, arresting both men and women and throwing them into prison, as also the high priest and all the Council can testify. I even obtained letters from them to their brothers in Damascus, and went there to bring these people as prisoners to Jerusalem to be punished.
(Acts 22:3–5)

Saul was on another mission. He was headed to Damascus in Syria to persecute the church, followers of the sect called the Way. He had letters from the high priest in Jerusalem to the synagogues in Damascus. He hoped these letters would help him arrest more Christians.

But Saul's life was about to change — radically. On the road to Damascus, Jesus appeared to Saul in a vision. There was a blinding light. Saul fell to the ground. He heard a voice from heaven: "Saul, Saul, why do you persecute me?"

Saul was stunned. He was convinced he had been pursuing the true God with every fiber of his being.

Suddenly, he realized he had been headed in the wrong direction.

The rest is history. As the latter part of verse 10 tells us, Jesus told him to go into Damascus and await orders. Saul obeyed. Saul's name was later changed, and we know him as the apostle Paul. He was a great missionary and writer of 25 percent of the New Testament under the guidance of the Holy Spirit.

Once Paul finally submitted to the Lord, God used this man in amazing ways to tell others about Christ.

Let's be honest. Submission is not a popular concept. Our natural bent as humans is to be in control. We want to be in charge of our lives and do things our way.

Years ago, a fast food chain ran a series of ads on television. The catch line was "Have it your way!" The ad seemed to work effectively as multiplied thousands made a beeline to the restaurant so they could have food "their way."

Nice thought, but God doesn't work that way. He never has, and He never will. He is the Author and Creator of the universe. He has created us in His love and mercy. He has made each one to love Him and to serve Him. We have purpose in life.

The starting point for each person is to submit to the authority and rule of our Heavenly Father. How? By accepting Jesus Christ as your Savior. He came to this world to save us from our sin. He died for you and me. By trusting in His Name we have forgiveness for our sin. But we have much more. We have the assurance of eternity with the Lord. We also have the power of the Holy Spirit to help us live out our lives on this earth in obedience to God.

But submission doesn't start and end with becoming a Christian. This is only the beginning. It's a lifelong process, and it's not easy. But it's God chosen route for us to be conformed to the image of His Son.

Military men and women know that basic training, regardless of the branch, is only the beginning. It gets the warrior started along the right path. Growth and development continue to occur throughout a career. Even generals and admirals continue to learn and develop. The Christian life is like this. This side of heaven, we never stop growing and learning.

Submission applies to every area of our lives. Submission to God also means relating to our fellow human beings with an attitude of humility. You can't name any kind of relationship with other people where submission doesn't apply — marriage, parenting, work, community, church, etc.

In the devotions that follow, I've tried to touch on just a

few of the different areas of submission. I encourage you to read and study the verses carefully. Then pray for God to help you, particularly in the areas where submission may be most difficult.

Let me assure you that every human being struggles with submission. It's wired into our sin nature. But know that submission is doable, but not in our own strength. We must depend on the Lord and the power of His Spirit.

Don't allow yourself to become discouraged with setbacks. On a given day, you may be able to submit beautifully up to a certain point. Then a test comes and you blow it. Join the crowd. We all fail in our efforts to submit. The key is not to quit. Keep trying! ■

Follow God's Way

The Lord said to Gideon, "With the three hundred men that lapped I will save you and give the Midianites into your hands. Let all the other men go, each to his own place." So Gideon sent the rest of the Israelites to their tents but kept the three hundred, who took over the provisions and trumpets of the others.
(Judges 7:7,8)

Good leaders become better leaders when they submit to the Lord. This can be difficult, especially when God's counsel seems to run counter to human logic.

Around 1200 B.C., the Lord chose Gideon to lead Israel against the Midianites, a fierce people who had been terrorizing Israel for years.

Gideon summoned 32,000 fighting men to go against the Midianite force, an army numbering 135,000.

But then a strange thing happened. The Lord told Gideon that the Israelite army had too many men. If successful, Israel would believe they had achieved victory in their own strength rather than in the Lord's strength. Gideon eventually reduced his forces to just 300 men.

Despite numbering only 300 soldiers, God led the Israelites to a resounding victory over the much larger Midianite army.

Be like Gideon. Follow God's way. ∎

Blowing Smoke

But the Lord said to Samuel, "Do not consider his appearance or his height, for I have rejected him. The Lord does not look at the things man looks at. Man looks at the outward appearance, but the Lord looks at the heart."
(1 Samuel 16:7)

You've heard the cliché some leaders use: "I just love to be with the troops!" You also know that the troops are not easily fooled. They figure out quickly whether or not a leader cares about them. Soldiers pay more attention to what leaders do than to what they say.

God is the same way — only He is never fooled. He knows our hearts. Playing games with God never works. He desires our love and obedience.

Are you a leader with a good heart and the right kind of motivation? Or are you "blowing smoke"? Troops know. So does God.

Be honest with yourself. Do you have heart problems? Are you struggling in your love and obedience toward the Lord, or even toward your soldiers?

Why don't you tell Him your struggles and ask for His help. In His mercy and grace, He will help you. ■

Fear Him

When one rules over men in righteousness, when he rules in the fear of God, he is like the light of morning at sunrise on a cloudless morning, like the brightness after rain that brings the grass from the earth.
(2 Samuel 23:3,4)

Military leadership doctrine requires that leaders have three principal ethical responsibilities: be a good role model, develop your subordinates ethically, and lead in such a way as to avoid putting your subordinates into ethical dilemmas.

The above is unquestionably true, but easier said than done. Most leaders begin with the best of intentions. However, competing goals within the same organization can sometimes make it difficult to decipher the best path to follow. These pressures make it challenging to do the right thing all the time.

God's Word gives some timeless advice that works even in the most difficult times. "Fear Him." Not out of terror, but because God is in charge. He knows what He is doing and deserves our allegiance.

By fearing God and doing what He wants done in every situation, you will not become victim to the fear of man. The result will provide the kind of ethical leadership your soldiers deserve and respect. ∎

Availability Over Capability

"So now, go. I am sending you to Pharaoh to bring my people the Israelites out of Egypt." But Moses said to God, "Who am I, that I should go to Pharaoh and bring the Israelites out of Egypt?" (Exodus 3:10,11)

God had just issued a FRAGO (Frag Order) to Moses. Moses staggered at the thought of being God's chosen leader for a rescue mission that would take two million Israelites out of Egypt. He felt totally inadequate for the task and voiced his doubts directly to the Lord.

History proves that Moses accomplished the mission anyway. But Moses didn't succeed on the merit of his own human leadership abilities. He obeyed God, and the Lord supplied the means, even to include the miraculous crossing of the Red Sea.

Ever feel overwhelmed by a mission God has assigned you to accomplish? Remember that He isn't limited by our capability. His power and resources are without limit. God spoke our universe into existence. He can do anything.

God desires followers who will submit to His authority and make themselves available for any mission He chooses to assign us.

Fear not. Our Heavenly Commander will provide you with the capability. ■

Set Apart

*I am the Lord your God; consecrate yourselves
and be holy, because I am holy.*
(Leviticus 11:44)

Many soldiers read this command of the Lord and
think it is impossible to accomplish as members of the
Armed Forces. This isn't the case at all.

Being "holy" or "consecrated" simply means
allowing yourself to be set apart to serve God.

Among the godliest personalities in the Bible are
those who were soldiers. Joshua and David were
outstanding military leaders in Old Testament times and
were commended by the Lord for living righteous and
holy lives.

In the New Testament, selected military leaders again
are cited as being godly followers. One example is in
Matthew 8 when Jesus commends a Roman centurion
for his faith. In Acts 10, Luke describes the soldier
Cornelius as being a devout and righteous man.

God has ordained all authority, including the military
services. He is looking for men and women who will
serve Him in this capacity.

In today's Armed Forces, many men and women have
made the decision to set themselves apart in service to
God — and they are doing just that.

It's up to you to decide. You can do it! The Lord will
help you. ■

Heart Attitude

All these people gave their gifts out of their wealth;
but she out of her poverty put in all she
had to live on.
(Luke 21:4)

While an offering is being taken in the temple, Jesus cuts through the outer appearance of things and causes people to look at their hearts. While the rich gave more materially, Jesus commends the poor widow for her generosity. He's really praising her for the attitude of her heart. She did the best she could.

Is the point here that we should give all we have to the poor? No! If that were true, we'd all need to be on welfare!

The message is this: As we serve God, He is more concerned with the attitude of our heart than He is with how much we give or what we do. Our material wealth, or lack of it, is not the major issue. It's a matter of the heart!

Perhaps reading this verse has caused you to think about your own heart. How's your attitude? In your giving and other service for God, do you do so wholeheartedly? Or are you holding back?

Try it. Step out and do your best. After all, Jesus gave His all for you. ■

Self-Control

*Like a city whose walls are broken down is a man
who lacks self-control.
(Proverbs 25:28)*

In Bible times, a city depended upon its outer walls
as a major fortification against enemy attack. If the
opposing force could penetrate the walls of the city,
defeat was certain.

Apply this thought to leadership in the military.
The leader who lacks self-control becomes like a
city without walls. If the one in charge loses control,
subordinates suffer and the organization loses focus. In
combat, this can have disastrous consequences.

Leadership studies have shown that almost 50 percent
of leadership failures occur with the leader himself.
The last few years are replete with examples of leaders,
both inside and outside the military, who have failed
because they couldn't exercise self-control.

Take this analogy one step further. Life's daily
situations demand control as well. A lack of self-
control and the anger that usually follows combine to
worsen almost any situation. Relationships suffer.

One important tip to remember: Self-control is not just
a matter of will; it requires strength beyond our own.

Don't give the devil a foothold. Submit to God and ask
Him to help you remain under the Spirit's leadership. ■

Servant Leadership in Action

> *Not so with you. Instead, whoever wants to become great among you must be your servant, and whoever wants to be first must be your slave — just as the Son of Man did not come to be served, but to serve, and to give his life as a ransom for many.*
> *(Matthew 20:26–28)*

Servant leadership continues to be a buzz word in many circles these days — in the corporate world, the church world, and even in the military. The truth is that servant leadership is talked about more than it is practiced.

The question asked most frequently might sound like this: What does servant leadership look like? More specifically, within the military context, can you cite a good example of servant leadership?

Very simply, "Yes, I can." I want to relate an event that occurred in the life of a good friend. His name is Steve Banach. He is an Army Colonel who serves in the Infantry. Steve has spent a good part of his career with special operations, and he definitely looks the part. He is physically imposing and looks like a warrior — square jaw, muscular build, and carries himself like an athlete. Not the guy most of us would want to encounter in a dark alley. Professionally, he has established himself as an outstanding infantry commander with a proven record in combat. The story that follows occurred a few years ago in Afghanistan when he was serving as a Lieutenant Colonel in the Rangers.

First, a little background. Steve served as the commander of a Ranger Battalion in Afghanistan on two different occasions in 2001 and 2002. His unit had conducted numerous special operation direct action missions in the Konar Province in Northeastern Afghanistan during the summer of 2002. The organization developed a good reputation within the local Afghan communities, and was generally viewed as a disciplined and well-trained combat force. As a result, the Ranger unit established a high level of trust with the local population, a factor that set the tone for this story.

In August 2002, an Afghan middle-aged father traveled from the vicinity of Asmar, which was located to the north of the Ranger forward operating base (FOB) in the Konar Province. Anyone who has been in Afghanistan understands how arduous and dangerous any ground movement in this country can be. The Rangers had experienced a number of near and far enemy ambushes as they traversed these routes, along with the ubiquitous improvised explosive device (IED) threat in their area of operations.

Serving Others

Nonetheless, the Afghan father toiled under the weighty task of moving his son by horse-drawn cart from his home, at least a four-hour ride by vehicle to the Ranger FOB. He came seeking medical care for his son who was close to death. The boy looked to be about 7 years old. The boy had burn injuries that covered 80 to 90 percent of his chest, abdomen, legs and hands. According to the father, the boy was trapped under the weight of the roof of their mud hut when it collapsed and subsequently pinned the him against the open cooking stove in their home. The boy sustained the burns and had a baseball-sized open, oozing wound in the center of his chest. His fingers on both hands were badly burned and had begun to heal together. The boy had begun to heal in the fetal position, and his right thigh was now stuck to his chest.

The boy's father approached the FOB and knocked on the metal door. One of the young Rangers opened the door. To his surprise the boy's father placed his son in the arms of the Ranger. The Ranger was startled by the act and turned first to his Ranger buddy, and then to his Ranger sergeant and asked for guidance. The Ranger leadership immediately grasped the urgency of the situation and moved the boy and his father to the battalion medical facility on the FOB and the physician's assistant (PA) began an immediate diagnosis. The PA finished his assessment and communicated immediately to LTC Banach and the Special Operations command leadership to whom the unit was assigned.

Within hours, LTC Banach made arrangements for a medical evacuation helicopter to transport the boy and his father to an Army field hospital at Bagram Air Base, located just to the north of Kabul, the country's capitol. Providentially, a plastic surgeon arrived at the Army field hospital the day after the boy was flown to Bagram. This doctor was able to perform the required surgeries. The boy spent a total of six weeks in the hospital and received three major operations, the combination of which gave him complete use of his legs and fingers.

Due to the high operational tempo on the battlefield, it was about three weeks before LTC Banach could get over to the hospital to visit the young boy and his father. In the interim, he ensured that his unit medical officers were checking on the young boy. When he finally arrived at the hospital, he navigated his way through all of the medical tents and arrived in a small recovery room. He saw the young boy asleep on an elevated stretcher and the boy's father sitting on the ground to the left of the child. The father quickly got to his feet and extended his hands. As LTC Banach extended his right hand, the man grasped the commander's hand with both of his hands and began to shake it profusely.

LTC Banach looked at the man and told him that his son looked good and that they were very happy to help him and his child. Tears began to fall down the father's cheeks. The commander was awestruck and simply told him that he had three children of his own and that he hoped that someone would show mercy on them if they were ever in a similar situation.

As the father and LTC Banach talked to one another, neither could understand what the other was saying. But the communication was perfect. LTC Banach could understand the father's deep emotion and thanks. The father could see that this American commander genuinely cared for him and his son.

In many respects it can be argued that war is simply a complete failure of mankind. But war was what brought this father and this commander together. In this one moment, each man stepped out of the stress and strain of war and shared a unique experience marked by peace and decency. It was a divinely ordained moment, one that showed the love and mercy of one human being to another.

Later, LTC Banach arranged to fly the boy and his father back to his FOB at Asadabad with a brand-new soccer ball and a couple of big bags of candy. Then, a few of his Rangers on the ground transported them back to their home near Asmar.

Today, neither LTC Banach nor any of the others involved in this experience know what has happened to this boy or his father. What they do know is that for a moment in time and in the most difficult circumstances imaginable, they had the privilege to participate in a true act of servanthood. ∎

Scars Like Jesus

Finally, let no one cause me trouble, for I bear on my body the marks of Jesus.
(Galatians 6:17)

Worthwhile endeavors in life usually cost you something. Few people know this truth better than soldiers. Cemeteries hold the bodies of many American soldiers who have made the ultimate sacrifice. Thousands of other soldiers wear the scars of war for life.

Spiritual warfare is no different. The apostle Paul tells us that service for his Commander, Jesus Christ, resulted in scars. His scars, rather than being a disgrace, bear testimony to the character of his service — dedicated, courageous, and selfless.

Some people mistakenly equate successful Christian living with avoidance of pain, suffering scars, or even an early death. The Bible reports otherwise. Experience supports this as well.

Know, however, that this verse is not referring to the pain, suffering, and scars we get from our own wrongdoing. Sin has its own set of consequences.

In the daily battles of life, serving God will bring resistance from the enemy. Wounds will come, but so will victories. When this happens, you will join the ranks of multiplied millions who have suffered for Jesus' sake. ■

Being a Servant

Each one should use whatever gift he has received to serve others, faithfully administering God,s grace in its various forms.
(1 Peter 4:10)

During the Revolutionary War, a large-framed man on a horse observed three privates struggling unsuccessfully to complete a log obstacle while a corporal stood by watching them. Despite the exhortations by their leader, they simply could not lift the heavy log into place.

The man on the horse asked the leader, "Why don't you help them?"

The reply: "You don't understand. I'm a corporal."

The man got down off his horse, removed his cape, and assisted the three men. The log went into place easily.

The man's name? General George Washington. He demonstrated his leadership by being a servant.

From God's perspective, leadership is not meant to be a matter of prestige, power, and control over others. Rather, leadership is influence for the purpose of helping the organization to accomplish its mission and helping those serving under you to maximize their God-given potential.

If you are a leader, or aspiring to become one, give thought to these words from Jesus. He led as a servant.

He calls us to do likewise. ■

Leadership Has Consequences

But the people did not listen. Manasseh led them astray, so that they did more evil than the nations the Lord had destroyed before the Israelites.
(2 Kings 21:9)

Leadership has consequences, and not just for the leader. Consequences impact those who follow — for good or for evil.

Rulers of nations wield enormous influence. In the case of Manasseh, king over Judah, the results were disastrous. Though he was the son of godly king Hezekiah, Manasseh did great evil in the sight of God. The people not only saw it; they also followed.

How bad was this evil? This chapter reports that Manasseh led the charge in worshipping idols, practicing divination and sorcery, and even sacrificing his own son in the fire. And the people? They did likewise.

Consider your own experiences. Have you noticed that good leaders make organizations better, and that poor leaders tend to take the organization down? Interestingly, this happens in every area of life, including the family.

Few of us will rule nations, but we do lead — on the job, in our communities, and in our homes. Rest assured that our leadership has consequences — for good or for evil. ∎

Day 4

Serving Wholeheartedly

*Serve wholeheartedly, as if you were serving the
Lord, not men, because you know that the Lord
will reward everyone for whatever good he does,
whether he is slave or free.
(Ephesians 6:7,8)*

In the workplace, military or civilian, one of the most
frequently asked questions sounds like this: "How do
you like your boss?" Often subordinates will cite poor
leadership as the reason they don't work harder.

This is not surprising. The leader in any environment
is important. Organizations succeed or fail largely on
the basis of leadership. In fact, survey data reports that
job satisfaction for most people hinges not on money,
but on one's relationship with or opinion of the boss.

Interestingly, the Bible takes another view. Christians
are to serve wholeheartedly whomever they work for.
The competency, popularity, or effectiveness of the
leader is not the issue.

Why? Because God commands us to do our best
regardless of our work situation. Ultimately, we are
serving Him. He sees what we are doing and will
reward us for our efforts.

Ask the Lord how you are doing toward supporting
your boss. Brace yourself. God will answer your
question. ■

The Good Samaritan

But a Samaritan, as he traveled, came where the man was; and when he saw him, he took pity on him. He went to him and bandaged his wounds, pouring on oil and wine. Then he put the man on his own donkey, took him to an inn and took care of him.
(Luke 10:33,34)

Jesus told this story in answer to a question: "Who is my neighbor." The man asking the question was trying to make himself look good. His strategy failed. Jesus exposed the man's heart.

Jesus' point in telling the parable was to highlight this truth: When it comes to caring for others, actions count. Not good intentions. Not words. And certainly not excuses.

Caring for others can be costly, risky, and messy — sometimes all three. All too often the nightly news will report a situation where a person is injured or mugged in a crowded area, but no one helps the victim. Why? Too costly, too risky, too messy.

True — we can't help every one. But as we accept this truth, the Lord will guide us to those fellow human beings whom we are supposed to help.

It's the right thing to do. ∎

Five Loaves and Two Fish

Another of his disciples, Andrew, Simon Peter's brother, spoke up, "Here is a boy with five small barley loaves and two small fish, but how far will they go among so many?"
(John 6:8,9)

Picture the scene. Jesus and the disciples have been ministering to thousands of people. They're tired and need rest. Only one problem. A crowd of 8,000 to 10,000 people is hungry and unable to feed themselves. They look to Jesus and the disciples to help.

The disciples weren't much help. They simply told Jesus the task was impossible. Andrew announced that a boy standing nearby was willing to donate five loaves and two fish to the cause.

Jesus told the disciples to seat the people. He took the five loaves and two fish, said a prayer, and ordered the disciples to distribute the food to the crowd.

It was a miracle! The people had plenty to eat, and there was even food left over. Jesus multiplied the efforts of a young boy who was willing to help others.

Do you wonder what Jesus would do with your efforts to help others? There is only one way to find out. Step out and serve. ∎

Whoever Wants To Be First

Not so with you. Instead, whoever wants to become great among you must be your servant, and whoever wants to be first must be slave of all.
(Mark 10:43,44)

Just look around. Is there any doubt that we live in a culture that says, "Me first"? Yes, this can even be true of the military when it comes to matters like promotions and assignments. We've all seen self-serving people.

Our Heavenly Commander in Chief has shared some definite guidance about service. Jesus spoke these words in answer to a request from two of His disciples, James and John. They boldly asked if they could sit on Jesus' right and left when Jesus comes into His full glory.

Jesus turned the tables on them, announcing that greatness in His kingdom would come from service, not status. Being first would only come from one's willingness to be the servant of all.

If you are a leader, Jesus' words mean this: The more people you lead, the more you serve. With higher rank come greater responsibilities and fewer rights. Leaders surrender privileges to serve those under their care.

Being a leader is no easy thing. It was never meant to be easy. ■

Knowing the Thief's Strategy

The thief comes only to steal and kill and destroy; I have come that they may have life, and have it to the full.
(John 10:10)

The question of whether Satan exists is one of the most contentious theological debates of our time. Discussions on this subject polarize people both inside and outside the Christian church.

Interestingly, this is not an issue in the Bible, neither Old or New Testament. From Genesis to Revelation, Satan is mentioned many times though not by the same name. Jesus often spoke about Satan in His teaching.

One of those teachings is found in John 10. Jesus is drawing a comparison. He refers to himself as the Good Shepherd. He refers to Satan as the thief: "The thief comes only to steal and kill and destroy."

If I know anything about life, I know that God is real. So is Satan. There is a heaven. Hell exists, too. Life is a struggle. We are engaged in a daily spiritual battle. Satan wants to destroy you whether you are a Christian or not. Jesus wants you to have life, and have it to the fullest measure possible.

The devil is a powerful enemy that we should not underestimate. In our own strength, we are no match for him.

But Jesus came to save us and to destroy the works of the devil. At the cross, He triumphed over Satan. By rising from the dead, Jesus conquered death, hell, and the grave. By faith in His name, we have forgiveness of our sins. We also have the power to stop sinning.

Though the war has been won, there are yet battles to be fought. Satan has not been totally subdued yet, and he is still raising havoc around the globe. Spiritual warfare is still ongoing.

Since we are engaged in this battle for our souls, it only makes sense to understand as much as we can about our enemy. That's why Jesus taught so much about Satan. He wanted His disciples and the people of that time to know the devil's strategy and tactics.

The devotions in this section aim to do just that. Remember that the Bible has much to say on this topic, and it's smart to make a study of the enemy's tactics a lifelong pursuit.

But I want to leave you with one powerful example. It happened to a good friend and fellow military chaplain. This story graphically illustrates the importance of knowing Satan's strategy and tactics as they apply to your own life.

Knowing Your Enemy

My friend, Jeff, returned from 15 hard months in Iraq. His unit experienced frequent combat with the enemy, and unfortunately lost many soldiers. Jeff ministered faithfully throughout the deployment and developed the reputation as a soldier's chaplain, one who was with them constantly and even during dangerous situations.

Even prior to his return from Iraq, I had spoken with Jeff on several occasions. I could tell that the effects of combat were taking a toll on him. I encouraged him to seek help.

Upon his return to the United States, Jeff's post traumatic stress became quite evident. We talked a few times, and to his credit, Jeff sought professional help. After a few months of counseling, he began to experience noticeable improvement. He was not out of the woods by any means, but his progress was encouraging.

Six months after his return to the U.S., he and his wife received orders to another post. He was going to work with a basic training unit. I was glad because I believed Jeff would excel with new recruits. Having been a former enlisted soldier himself, he could relate with their challenges. As a proven combat veteran, he could also help these trainees prepare for the rigors of war.

Jeff and his wife moved to their new assignment. Things started off very well. Jeff loved his ministry, they liked the area, and Jeff's chain of command knew they had an outstanding chaplain on their team.

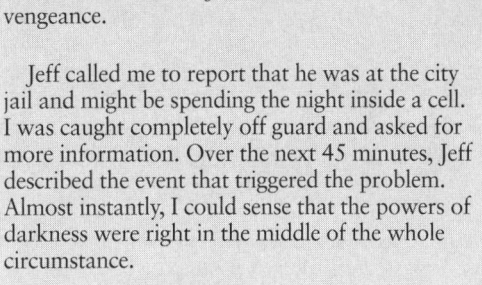

Remember the thief. With him, no one is off limits. The stronger your Christian witness, the more Satan wants to destroy you. I believe he went after Jeff with a vengeance.

Jeff called me to report that he was at the city jail and might be spending the night inside a cell. I was caught completely off guard and asked for more information. Over the next 45 minutes, Jeff described the event that triggered the problem. Almost instantly, I could sense that the powers of darkness were right in the middle of the whole circumstance.

Jeff had been walking with his 9-month pregnant wife along the road in their neighborhood. Their dog was with them. With no sidewalks, they were forced to walk along the right side of the road.

Suddenly a car came roaring up the road from behind, almost hitting them. They leaped to the side of the road. Jeff screamed at the car to slow down. It had been a close call. His wife was scared. Jeff was scared, too, but mostly angry.

To their surprise, the car stopped on the hill in front of them. The driver put the car in reverse and came back toward them with amazing speed. Again, they leaped off the side of the road. The car stopped and the driver jumped out.

Jeff, both scared and angry, did not know what to expect next. He reached into his pocket and pulled out his pocketknife in case the driver might try to hurt them.

Fortunately, there was no physical contact. But there were shouts and threats coming from both Jeff and the woman who had been driving. After exchanging harsh words, the woman got back into her car and drove off.

The next day Jeff went to the local sheriff's office to file a report. To his surprise, the woman had beaten him to the punch. Her account and his account of the incident could not have been more different. She was filing criminal charges. The whole situation was about to get serious.

I will spare you most of the details, except to say this. With each passing day, the case seemed to get uglier. The lady's intent was clearly to destroy Jeff. She made her way around to almost every neighbor and even got a friend to go to Jeff's house to threaten him. Lies were spread. The situation was toxic.

When the dust settled and lawyers on both sides compared notes, it was clear that the prosecution wanted to end Jeff's career as a chaplain, and possibly to put him in prison for a long time.

When Satan gets involved, the only rule is that there are no rules. Untruths were spread to senior chaplains on the installation, and word of the charges appeared in the national news. The negatives against Jeff, true or not, were stacking up rapidly.

The challenge for a military chaplain in this situation is that a "near win" would not suffice. Anything less than full exoneration could likely end Jeff's career.

But lest we give Satan too much credit, read the second part of verse 10 above. Jesus says He has "come that they may have life, and have it to the full."

As only He could, the Lord helped Jeff locate a witness who saw the whole incident and knew of other instances where the lady had tried to hurt people. Additionally, the Lord helped Jeff's attorney present a powerful defense to a grand jury that resulted in the case being completely thrown out of court.

Jeff called me and related the good news. Of course I celebrated with him. But as we reviewed the happenings, we both saw the enemy's hand in all of this. Was Jeff happy with the lady? Of course not. She had lied and tried to destroy Jeff and his family. But behind her actions, we saw the enemy at work. The apostle Paul states it so beautifully in Ephesians:

*For our struggle is not against flesh and blood,
but against the rulers, against the authorities,
against the powers of this dark world and against
the spiritual forces of evil in the heavenly realms.
(Ephesians 6:12)*

Bottom line: Know your enemy — his strategy and tactics. With God's help, you can defeat him. ■

Knowing the Enemy

> *Be self-controlled and alert. Your enemy the devil prowls around like a roaring lion looking for someone to devour. Resist him, standing firm in the faith, because you know that your brothers throughout the world are undergoing the same kind of sufferings.*
> *(1 Peter 5:8,9)*

Military commanders use the IPB (Intelligence Preparation of the battlefield) process in planning strategy against the enemy. They recognize the importance of knowing the enemy — who he is, what his forces are, how he plans to fight, etc. — as being key for victory.

Spiritual warfare is no different. We must recognize that people and nations are not really our enemy. The real enemy is Satan along with his demonic forces who oppose God and anyone who tries to follow God's ways. His strategy can be lethal.

It may come as a surprise to many, but Satan uses his own IPB process in warring against our souls. If you look around at our world today, it's obvious that he is being very successful.

Your life is important. Don't let the enemy outmaneuver you. Know your spiritual opponent. By knowing your enemy and using the right strategy, the Bible assures us that we can defeat the "enemy of our souls." ■

Contending for Truth

Dear friends, although I was very eager to write to you about the salvation we share, I felt I had to write and urge you to contend for the faith that was once for all entrusted to the saints.
(Jude 3)

Jude, the writer of this verse, warns Christians to contend for their faith. In later verses he explains that there are evil men who use religion solely for selfish motives. These men are godless, dangerous, and destined for destruction.

Times haven't changed. As warriors, we contend for freedom and the things that are right. Numerous times in our nation's history we've had to resort to force. Many of our patriots have paid the price for freedom with their blood.

In the spiritual realm, the battle for truth is not any easier. As Jude warns in this verse, Christians must contend for it. Contending involves struggle, and struggle is often hard.

You may not become a martyr, but this doesn't mean you won't have to contend for the truth. A good starting place is in God's Word. Read it, study it, meditate on it, and obey it. If you do, you will surely keep the faith entrusted to you. ■

Keep Watch

Then he returned to his disciples and found them sleeping. "Could you men not keep watch with me for one hour?" He asked Peter.
(Matthew 26:40)

Most soldiers know how difficult staying awake on guard duty can be, especially during the hours of darkness. History has proven, though, that failure to remain awake and alert has cost lives in every war.

As an infantry lieutenant in Vietnam, I routinely pulled guard from 3 to 6 a.m. As the leader, I felt accountable and responsible to make sure all soldiers performing guard stayed alert.

In the spiritual war for our souls, the enemy hopes to find us asleep. This verse is a vivid reminder of how easily we can let our spiritual guard down. Peter, James, and John failed to keep watch with Jesus for just one hour.

Understanding the enemy's strategy and tactics can motivate us to be more watchful. For example, predators have abducted children when parents didn't keep watch. Simple attentiveness could have averted disaster. It works that way in our struggle against the devil as well.

Can the Lord count on you to "keep watch" spiritually? Your very soul depends on it. ■

False Apostles of Christ

For such men are false apostles, deceitful workmen, masquerading as apostles of Christ. And no wonder, for Satan himself masquerades as an angel of light.
(2 Corinthians 11:13,14)

With strong language the apostle Paul tells Christians in Corinth that there are false apostles in their midst. He describes them as deceitful men who masquerade as though Christ sent them.

Are there false apostles in the world today? Definitely, and here's one example. Some teachers and preachers would have you think that living the Christian life, if done correctly, leads to jumping from one mountaintop to the next. No down times. No sickness. No financial hardships. No depression. No suffering.

Think about this. Do you know anyone who lives like this? I don't. Being a follower of Jesus does not insulate us from hard times.

But how can we discern the truth and know which people are pedaling a false gospel? We have God's truth — the Holy Bible. We should read it, study it, and obey it. We should also make certain the preaching and teaching we hear lines up with God's Word. If it doesn't, it's false teaching.

We don't need to be deceived. Follow Christ and His Word. ∎

Don't Give the Devil a Foothold

"In your anger do not sin": Do not let the sun go down while you are still angry, and do not give the devil a foothold.
(Ephesians 4:26,27)

A popular notion today is that we have the right to speak out about anything, anytime, anywhere, and to anyone. This especially applies to anger. It's "no holds barred." In fact, television networks abound with programs where people display anger with reckless abandon.

God looks at anger differently. Granted, anger is a God-given emotion. We all experience it. Numerous references in Scripture talk about God's righteous anger. Even Jesus got angry, especially at hypocritical, self-righteous religious leaders.

But for the most part, man's anger needs to be kept in check. These verses don't tell us not to be angry. Rather, they warn us not to permit our anger to lead to sin.

Why? At the practical level, little good ever comes from such anger. But there is another reason. Anger that leads to sin gives our enemy a foothold. He can use our anger to serve his many evil purposes, one of which is to tarnish our Christian witness.

Play it smart. Don't give the devil a foothold. ∎

You Will Not Die

> *"You will not surely die," the serpent said to the*
> *woman. "For God knows that when you eat of it*
> *your eyes will be opened, and you will be like God,*
> *knowing good and evil."*
> *(Genesis 3:4,5)*

Spiritual warfare is real. Satan is real. He wants to destroy you.

Our archenemy can defeat us if we don't understand his strategy and tactics. His oldest tactic appears in these verses.

Satan, disguised as a serpent, is talking to Eve. He is tempting her to disobey God's command found in Genesis 2:16,17 — "You are free to eat from any tree in the garden; but you must not eat from the tree of the knowledge of good and evil, for when you eat of it you will surely die."

Notice the devil's strategy. He tells two lies. First, he tells Eve she won't die. Second, he tells Eve that if she eats the fruit she will become like God.

What is Satan's point? First, he is accusing God of being a liar. Second, he is tempting Eve to doubt God's goodness and to believe God is withholding blessing from her and her husband.

Don't believe Satan. God is good. The devil is a liar. ∎

The Accuser of Our Brothers

Then I heard a loud voice in heaven say: "Now have come the salvation and the power and the kingdom of our God, and the authority of his Christ. For the accuser of our brothers, who accuses them before our God day and night, has been hurled down."
(Revelation 12:10)

One of the names of our spiritual enemy is the "accuser." He has been accusing for thousands of years.

How does he accuse us? Consider the following lies:

- We have sinned so much that God won't forgive us.
- We will never amount to anything.
- God is not real. We are chasing a fantasy.
- God will not hear our prayers.
- We are hypocrites.
- We'll never be able to overcome our sinful habits.

Unfortunately, the accuser has been all too successful, even against Christians. Perhaps you can identify times when the accuser has hurt you.

So what can we do? We can choose to believe God and His Word. This verse tells us that the accuser has been hurled out of heaven. He has lost his place.

Jesus rules. The accuser has been defeated. We win. Now live like it. ∎

Working Together for Good

And we know that in all things God works for the good of those who love him, who have been called according to his purpose.
(Romans 8:28)

It's no secret that we live in a fallen world.

Though everything God created in the beginning was good, mankind has continued to mess up. This holds true especially in relationships, both at the personal and national level. I'm talking about the way people treat each other. Just watch the news and read the paper. It's heartbreaking to us, and I'm sure even more to God.

Fortunately, things can change. People can choose to help others, especially in difficult situations. In fact, I've noticed that when we try to support people who are experiencing hard times, God has a way of multiplying the good that we do. Let me illustrate.

A few years ago, I was assigned as the pastor for Hannam Village Chapel in Seoul, South Korea. Hannam was the largest U.S. government-owned housing area in Korea, containing approximately 5,000 military and family members.

To contain that many people in a relatively small geographical space, the government had built large buildings, several of which were 15 stories high. In addition to housing, the government had built

other facilities to support a
population of that size — not
luxurious by any stretch, but
certainly adequate. All in all,
life in Hannam was pretty good.
Understandably, though, relationships in that
crowded community were often strained.

One evening a fire broke out in a housing
unit on the 15th floor of a high-rise building.
I don't recall what caused the fire, but the
flames grew quickly and threatened to destroy
the top floor, and even the entire building. The
occupants of the unit were not home when the
blaze started.

It looked like a crisis scene from a movie.
Fortunately, neighbors responded quickly
and initiated emergency procedures. The occupants
evacuated the building rapidly while the fire department
rushed to the scene. Two fire trucks raised giant ladders
to the top of the building. Firemen quickly hosed down
the apartment inside and out and managed to contain
the fire to the one unit. However, that apartment had
been devastated. The family could not salvage any
of their personal belongings, much less any of their
furniture. They suffered total loss of their possessions,
but counted themselves fortunate to have escaped with
their lives.

People who have lost everything in fire suffer much
more than most of us realize. Practically, the family

must start from scratch. Things like furniture and clothes can be replaced. Other belongings like pictures, letters and special keepsakes cannot. The sense of loss is off the charts.

But God had triumph in store for this situation. Romans 8:28 tells us that God is able to work all things together for good for those who love Him and are called according to His purpose. It doesn't say everything that happens is good, nor that things automatically work out for good. Some intentionality is required.

The Hannam Village community became intentional quickly. Neighbors rallied to find the family a place to stay and get a few essentials. As the chaplain, I worked with the community mayor and other leaders in an effort to research available resources within the local community and from formal helping agencies within the military. We took great care to communicate with the family to insure the support being offered was both needed and desired.

Government housing authorities located another permanent place for the family to live at Hannam. Volunteers stepped up to locate furniture and all kinds of household articles and furnishings to turn the apartment into a home. Members from our chapel provided the major impetus for the overwhelming response to the family, a fact that surprised family members since they were not chapel attendees.

The list of actions needed to reestablish a home from the ground up is staggering, and far too numerous to mention here. It is sufficient to say that for every need the family had, a volunteer cheerfully provided the necessary assistance.

While nothing could erase the pain of the family's loss, God brought His comfort through people. In both word and deed the community showed love, compassion, and emotional support to each member of the family. The family responded beautifully, displaying amazing resilience in the face of adversity. Within two weeks, they had made great progress toward normal living.

Still, this situation needed a sense of formal closure, both for the family and the community. Leaders worked together to plan an event that could make this a reality. Unanimously, we voted to host a celebration for the entire village. We had much for which to give thanks and celebrate.

The occasion went off without a hitch. From the youngest to the oldest, we were surprised at the joy present that day. Food, games, prizes, music, speeches, and prayers were just a few of the activities. We closed by collecting a special offering for the family. People gave with glad hearts.

Now years later, I vividly remember God's mercy and goodness in that potentially deadly situation, not only to the family but to all of us. A genuine team effort put a family back together after a disaster.

But the change the Lord brought to the people of Hannam Village proved to be transformational. People were friendlier and more helpful to each other. Interest in community activities picked up dramatically, and the overall mood across Hannam Village noticeably improved. Even people from other military housing areas viewed the people of our community with new respect. Local military commanders expressed repeated thanks for accomplishing something no military order could have produced.

And one more thing. God was glorified. Week after week visitors piled into Hannam Chapel to find out what made chapel folks so loving and giving. Many stayed and became active members of our congregation. Americans and Koreans worshipped God together, praising Him, growing in faith, and spreading the Word that God can truly work all things together for good.

Facing a tough situation or even a crisis? Let God work all things together for good. ■

Victory Over Jealousy

*As they danced, they sang: "Saul has slain his
thousands, and David his tens of thousands."
Saul was very angry; this refrain galled him.
"They have credited David with tens of thousands,"
he thought, "but me with only thousands. What
more can he get but the kingdom?"*
(1 Samuel 18:7,8)

Jealousy is a green-eyed monster whose specialty is
wrecking lives. Jealousy can thrive in any community,
including the military.

These verses focus on two military leaders, Saul and
David. Angered over David's military successes and
popularity with the people, Saul allowed jealousy to
destroy his career and his walk with God.

Jealousy still destroys lives today. At its core, jealousy
is telling God that what He has provided is not good
enough. Jealous people do some horrible things. Some
have even murdered. Bottom line: Nothing good comes
out of jealousy.

Our Heavenly Commander provides a sure way
to defeat this monster. How? Through an attitude of
thankfulness. A thankful attitude focuses our attention
on what we have — not on what we don't have.

Don't let jealousy defeat you. Take the upper hand by
giving thanks to the Lord with a grateful heart! ■

Harsh Words

A gentle answer turns away wrath, but a harsh word stirs up anger.
(Proverbs 15:1)

Some leaders believe the myth that sharp words and harsh tones get better results from subordinates. During a firefight this may be true. However, most other times this approach is not smart.

We have all witnessed scenes where a leader has used harsh words in an effort to get better results from subordinates. This not only doesn't work most of the time, but it has other detrimental effects as well. First, it can humiliate followers. Second, it sets a bad example, and certainly is not the way we should train future leaders.

The Bible tells us that harsh words stir up anger. Anger has some place in our lives, but usually the results are negative rather than positive. Gentleness and respect in speech turns away wrath and usually gets better results from soldiers.

But this truth is not confined to the military setting. It applies in virtually every setting. It applies especially to the home.

So think about it. The next time you are about to blow someone away with your words, remember the truth of this verse. It works! ∎

Forgiveness

*If you, O Lord, kept a record of sins, O Lord, who
could stand? But with you there is forgiveness;
therefore you are feared.
(Psalm 130:3)*

As long as the military remains a relatively small,
volunteer force, competition for promotion grows
tougher. Some feel that the military is moving toward a
"zero defects" mentality.

Results of recent selection boards for promotion,
leadership billets, and schooling reflect that many
quality people are not making the cut. Often the
difference between selection and nonselection is a
minor glitch in the individual's personnel record.

Fortunately, our Heavenly Commander has a
different personnel system. Our mistakes — and we all
make them — are tossed out of our Spiritual Personnel
File by the Commander Himself when we ask and
receive forgiveness.

Even though God promises forgiveness, some people
struggle with forgiving themselves. A few think this is
being humble. But it's not. It's actually running counter
to God's commands. Failure to forgive yourself has no
positive outcomes.

Are you burdened by the weight of your sins? Don't
delay! Confess your sins to the Lord and ask for His
forgiveness. He will set you free! ■

Becoming a Balcony Person

When [Saul] came to Jerusalem, he tried to join the disciples, but they were all afraid of him, not believing that he really was a disciple. But Barnabas took him and brought him to the apostles. He told them how Saul on his journey had seen the Lord and that the Lord had spoken to him, and how in Damascus he had preached fearlessly in the name of Jesus.
(Acts 9:26,27)

One of the most effective ways to enhance your relationships with people is to become an encourager, a balcony person — one who lifts others up.

Even though Paul was preaching and teaching the Christian message effectively, the disciples in Jerusalem questioned his credibility. They vividly remembered how Paul, then called Saul, had persecuted Christians.

But along came Barnabas. This godly man risked his own reputation and commended Paul to the disciples as one who should be accepted into their ranks as a brother in Christ.

His influence carried the day for Paul. Had this not occurred, perhaps Paul might never have become the great apostle and missionary who carried the gospel to the Gentile world.

What about you? Are you an encourager? If not, why not? ■

Show a Little Kindness

David asked, "Is there anyone still left of the house of Saul to whom I can show kindness for Jonathan's sake?"
(2 Samuel 9:1)

In today's fast-paced world, there is often a missing ingredient in our relationships — kindness.

There is a beautiful story in the Old Testament that illustrates the power of kindness. It's the story of King David and Mephibosheth. David's kindness was extraordinary for several reasons.

First, Mephibosheth was the grandson of Israel's former ruler, King Saul, a man who had acted viciously toward David and even tried to kill him.

Mephibosheth had another good reason to be afraid. It was usual in the ancient Middle East for founders of new dynasties to kill the children of former rulers to keep them from trying to regain the throne in the name of their families.

Finally, due to a childhood accident, Mephibosheth was crippled and could not walk. He could not do anything to give back to David for the king's kindness.

Becoming a kind person is a matter of choice. Kindness toward others reflects God's love, the kind of love that expects nothing in return. ∎

Building Relationships Through Church

They devoted themselves to the apostles' teaching and to the fellowship, to the breaking of bread and to prayer.
(Acts 2:42)

Among Christians during recent years, I have noticed two seemingly opposing trends.

The first trend is to stop attending church. The rationale goes something like this: "I don't have to go to church to be a Christian. I need more time to relax. Besides, I don't really like spending time with people I don't know."

On the other side of the coin, millions of people, including many Christians, are starving for relationships and spending increasingly greater amounts of time doing social networking through Facebook, My Space, and Twitter. Still, many wonderful Christian people are feeling lonely and isolated.

God has a great answer. It's called church. Many great things happen at church, especially toward developing solid, wholesome relationships with other people.

Will church involvement take initiative and effort on your part? Yes. Are the results worth it? Speaking personally, I have met some of the finest people on the planet. Where? In chapels and churches. ∎

Practice the Golden Rule

Do to others as you would have them do to you.
(Luke 6:31)

Relationships within the military environment can be tough at times. In certain respects, this is understandable.

The military is highly mission-oriented, and ultimately, the main purpose is to win our nation's wars. Unchecked, this can foster a climate that tends to reward behavior that is task-oriented, not people-oriented.

However, the greatest resource in any organization, military or otherwise, is people. It is essential to treat one another with respect. As America becomes more culturally diverse, military leaders must be aware that they will deal with people from a wider range of ethnic, racial, and religious backgrounds. Respect is a universal language.

But this is nothing new. In His Sermon on the Mount, Jesus identifies the key to having good relationships with others. Paraphrased, He simply tells us to treat others as we would like to be treated.

As simple as this principle sounds, doing it is not always so easy. People can be difficult.

At a personal level, a good place to start might be to ask yourself and the Lord this question: "Do I treat all people with respect?" ∎

All-Knowing (Omniscient)

Psalm 139:1–6

O Lord, you have searched me and you know me. You know when I sit and when I rise; you perceive my thoughts from afar. You discern my going out and my lying down; you are familiar with all my ways. Before a word is on my tongue you know it completely, O Lord. You hem me in — behind and before; you have laid your hand upon me. Such knowledge is too wonderful for me, too lofty for me to attain.

Proverbs 5:21

For a man's ways are in full view of the Lord, and he examines all his paths.

All-Powerful (Omnipotent)

Job 37:23

The Almighty is beyond our reach and exalted in power.

Matthew 28:18

Then Jesus came to them and said, "All authority in heaven and on earth has been given to me."

Revelation 19:6

Then I heard what sounded like a great multitude, like the roar of rushing waters and like loud peals of thunder, shouting: "Hallelujah! For our Lord God Almighty reigns."

Compassionate

Exodus 34:6

And he passed in front of Moses, proclaiming, "The Lord, the Lord, the compassionate and gracious God, slow to anger, abounding in love and faithfulness."

Psalm 86:15

But you, O Lord, are a compassionate and gracious God, slow to anger, abounding in love and faithfulness.

Psalm 116:5

The Lord is gracious and righteous; our God is full of compassion.

Creative

Genesis 1:1

In the beginning God created the heavens and the earth.

John 1:3

Through him all things were made; without him nothing was made that has been made.

Eternal

Deuteronomy 33:27

The eternal God is your refuge, and underneath are the everlasting arms.

Isaiah 26:4

Trust in the Lord forever, for the Lord, the Lord, is the Rock eternal.

1 Timothy 1:17

Now to the King eternal, immortal, invisible, the only God, be honor and glory for ever and ever. Amen.

Ever-Present (Omnipresent)

Psalm 139:7

Where can I go from your Spirit? Where can I flee from your presence?

Jeremiah 23:23

"Am I only a God nearby," declares the Lord, "and not a God far away?"

Faithful

1 Corinthians 1:9

God, who has called you into fellowship with his Son Jesus Christ our Lord, is faithful.

1 Corinthians 10:13

No temptation has seized you except what is common to man. And God is faithful; he will not let you be tempted beyond what you can bear. But when you are tempted, he will also provide a way out so that you can stand up under it.

1 Thessalonians 5:24

The one who calls you is faithful and he will do it.

2 Thessalonians 3:3

But the Lord is faithful, and he will strengthen and protect you from the evil one.

Hebrews 3:6

But Christ is faithful as a son over God's house. And we are his house, if we hold on to our courage and the hope of which we boast.

1 Peter 4:19

So then, those who suffer according to God's will should commit themselves to their faithful Creator and continue to do good.

Glorious

Exodus 15:11

Who among the gods is like you, O Lord? Who is like you—majestic in holiness, awesome in glory, working wonders?

Psalm 145:5

They will speak of the glorious splendor of your majesty, and I will meditate on your wonderful works.

Good

Psalm 25:8

Good and upright is the Lord; therefore he instructs sinners in his ways.

Psalm 119:68

You are good, and what you do is good; teach me your decrees.

Gracious

2 Kings 13:23

But the Lord was gracious to them and had compassion and showed concern for them because of his covenant with Abraham, Isaac and Jacob. To this day he has been unwilling to destroy them or banish them from his presence.

Joel 2:13

Rend your heart and not your garments. Return to the Lord your God, for he is gracious and compassionate, slow to anger and abounding in love, and he relents from sending calamity.

Great

Deuteronomy 7:21

Do not be terrified by them, for the Lord your God, who is among you, is a great and awesome God.

2 Chronicles 2:5

The temple I am going to build will be great, because our God is greater than all other gods.

Psalm 86:10

For you are great and do marvelous deeds; you alone are God.

1 John 4:4

You, dear children, are from God and have overcome them, because the one who is in you is greater than the one who is in the world.

Holy

Exodus 15:11

Who among the gods is like you, O Lord? Who is like you—majestic in holiness, awesome in glory, working wonders?

Psalm 99:9

Exalt the Lord our God and worship at his holy mountain for the Lord our God is holy.

1 Peter 1:15,16

But just as he who called you is holy, so be holy in all you do; for it is written: "Be holy, because I am holy."

Immortal

1 Timothy 1:17

Now to the King eternal, immortal, invisible, the only God, be honor and glory for ever and ever. Amen.

1 Timothy 6:16

Who alone is immortal and who lives in unapproachable light, whom no one has seen or can see. To him be honor and might forever. Amen.

Invisible

Job 23:8,9

But if I go to the east, he is not there; if I go to the west, I do not find him. When he is at work in the north, I do not see him; when he turns to the south, I catch no glimpse of him.

John 1:18

No one has ever seen God, but God the One and Only, who is at the Father's side, has made him known.

Colossians 1:15

He is the image of the invisible God, the firstborn over all creation.

1 Timothy 1:17

Now to the King eternal, immortal, invisible, the only God, be honor and glory for ever and ever. Amen.

Jealous:

Exodus 20:3

You shall have no other gods before me.

Joshua 24:19

Joshua said to the people, "You are not able to serve the Lord. He is a holy God; he is a jealous God. He will not forgive your rebellion and your sins."

Nahum 1:2

The Lord is a jealous and avenging God: the Lord takes vengeance and is filled with wrath. The Lord takes vengeance on his foes and maintains his wrath against his enemies.

Just

Deuteronomy 32:4

He is the Rock, his works are perfect, and all his ways are just. A faithful God who does no wrong, upright and just is he.

2 Thessalonians 1:6

God is just: He will pay back trouble to those who trouble you.

Revelation 19:11

I saw heaven standing open and there before me was a white horse, whose rider is called Faithful and True. With justice he judges and makes war.

Kind

Job 10:12

You gave me life and showed me kindness, and in your providence watched over my spirit.

Isaiah 54:8

"In a surge of anger I hid my face from you for a moment, but with everlasting kindness I will have compassion on you," says the Lord your Redeemer.

Titus 3:4,5

But when the kindness and love of God our Savior appeared, he saved us, not because of righteous things we had done, but because of his mercy.

Light

Isaiah 60:19

The sun will no more be your light by day, for the Lord will be your everlasting light, and your God will be your glory.

John 1:4

In him was life, and that life was the light of men.

James 1:17

Every good and perfect gift is from above, coming down from the Father of the heavenly lights, who does not change like shifting shadows.

Long-suffering

1 Timothy 1:16

But for that very reason I was shown mercy so that in me, the worst of sinners, Christ Jesus might display his unlimited patience as an example for those who would believe on him and receive eternal life.

2 Peter 3:9

The Lord is not slow in keeping his promise, as some understand slowness. He is patient with you, not wanting anyone to perish, but everyone to come to repentance.

Love

John 3:16

For God so loved the world that he gave his one and only Son, that whoever believes in him shall not perish but have eternal life.

Romans 5:8

But God demonstrates his own love for us in this: While we were still sinners, Christ died for us.

Romans 8:37–39

No, in all these things we are more than conquerors through him who loved us. For I am convinced that neither death nor life, neither angels nor demons, neither the present nor the future, nor any powers, neither height nor depth, nor anything else in all creation, will be able to separate us from the love of God that is in Christ Jesus our Lord.

Galatians 2:20

I have been crucified with Christ and I no longer live, but Christ lives in me. The life I live in the body, I live by faith in the Son of God, who loved me and gave himself for me.

1 John 4:7,8

Dear friends, let us love one another, for love comes from God. Everyone who loves has been born of God and knows God. Whoever does not love does not know God, because God is love.

Merciful

Jeremiah 3:12

Go, proclaim this message toward the north:
"Return, faithless Israel," declares the Lord,
"I will frown on you no longer,
for I am merciful," declares the Lord,
"I will not be angry forever."

Daniel 9:9

The Lord our God is merciful and forgiving, even though we have rebelled against him.

Most High

Psalm 83:18

Let them know that you, whose name is the Lord — that you alone are the Most High over all the earth.

Righteous

Ezra 9:15

O Lord, God of Israel, you are righteous! We are left this day as a remnant. Here we are before you in our guilt, though because of it not one of us can stand in your presence.

Psalm 145:17

The Lord is righteous in all his ways and loving toward all he has made.

2 Timothy 4:8

Now there is in store for me the crown of righteousness, which the Lord, the righteous Judge, will award to me on that day — and not only to me, but also to all who have longed for his appearing.

Spirit

John 4:24

God is spirit, and his worshipers must worship in spirit and in truth.

2 Corinthians 3:17

Now the Lord is the Spirit, and where the Spirit of the Lord is, there is freedom.

True

Jeremiah 10:10

But the Lord is the true God; he is the living God, the eternal King. When he is angry, the earth trembles; the nations cannot endure his wrath.

John 14:6

Jesus answered, "I am the way and the truth and the life. No one comes to the Father except through me."

John 17:3

Now this is eternal life: that they may know you, the only true God, and Jesus Christ, whom you have sent.

Unchanging

Psalm 102:26,27

They will perish, but you remain; they will all wear out like a garment. Like clothing you will change them and they will be discarded. But you remain the same, and your years will never end.

James 1:17

Every good and perfect gift is from above, coming down from the Father of the heavenly lights, who does not change like shifting shadows.

Unsearchable

Job 11:7

Can you fathom the mysteries of God? Can you probe the limits of the Almighty?

Romans 11:33

Oh, the depth of the riches of the wisdom and knowledge of God! How unsearchable his judgments, and his paths beyond tracing out!

Upright

Psalm 25:8

Good and upright is the Lord; therefore he instructs sinners in his ways.

The Bible is Divinely Inspired
2 Timothy 3:16,17
All Scripture is God-breathed and is useful for teaching, rebuking, correcting and training in righteousness, so that the man of God may be thoroughly equipped for every good work.

2 Peter 1:21
For prophecy never had its origin in the will of man, but men spoke from God as they were carried along by the Holy Spirit.

Reveals God's Laws and Statutes
Deuteronomy 4:5
See, I have taught you decrees and laws as the Lord my God commanded me, so that you may follow them in the land you are entering to take possession of it.

Psalm 119:9
How can a young man keep his way pure? By living according to your word.

Psalm 119:17,18
Do good to your servant, and I will live; I will obey your word. Open my eyes that I may see wonderful things in your law.

Psalm 119:30

I have chosen the way of truth; I have set my heart on your laws.

The Holy Spirit Helps Us to Understand Scripture

John 16:13

But when he, the Spirit of truth, comes, he will guide you into all truth. He will not speak on his own; he will speak only what he hears, and he will tell you what is yet to come.

1 Corinthians 2:9–14

However, as it is written: "No eye has seen, no ear has heard, no mind has conceived what God has prepared for those who love him" — but God has revealed it to us by his Spirit. The Spirit searches all things, even the deep things of God. For who among men knows the thoughts of a man except the man's spirit within him? In the same way no one knows the thoughts of God except the Spirit of God. We have not received the spirit of the world but the Spirit who is from God, that we may understand what God has freely given us. This is what we speak, not in words taught us by human wisdom but in words taught by the Spirit, expressing spiritual truths in spiritual words. The man without the Spirit does not accept the things that come from the Spirit of God, for they are foolishness to him, and he cannot understand them, because they are spiritually discerned.

Testifies to the Person and Work of Jesus Christ

John 5:39

You diligently study the Scriptures because you think that by them you possess eternal life. These are the Scriptures that testify about me.

Acts 10:43

All the prophets testify about him that everyone who believes in him receives forgiveness of sins through his name.

1 Corinthians 15:3

For what I received I passed on to you as of first importance: that Christ died for our sins according to the Scriptures, that he was buried, that he was raised on the third day according to the Scriptures, and that he appeared to Peter, and then to the Twelve.

Written for Use by All Men

Romans 16:25–27

Now to him who is able to establish you by my gospel and the proclamation of Jesus Christ, according to the revelation of the mystery hidden for long ages past, but now revealed and made known through the prophetic writings by the command of the eternal God, so that all

nations might believe and obey him — to the only wise
God be glory forever through Jesus Christ! Amen.

Nothing Should Be Added or Subtracted

Deuteronomy 4:2

Do not add to what I command you and do not
subtract from it, but keep the commands of the Lord
your God that I give you.

Revelation 22:18,19

I warn everyone who hears the words of the prophecy
of this book: If anyone adds anything to them, God
will add to him the plagues described in this book.
And if anyone takes words away from this book of
prophecy, God will take away from him his share in
the tree of life and in the holy city, which are described
in this book.

God's Word Has Many Names

Word

James 1:21,22

Therefore, get rid of all moral filth and the evil that is
so prevalent and humbly accept the word planted in
you, which can save you. Do not merely listen to the
word, and so deceive yourselves. Do what it says.

Sword of the Spirit
Ephesians 6:17

Take the helmet of salvation and the sword of the Spirit, which is the word of God.

Holy Scriptures
Romans 1:2

The gospel he promised beforehand through his prophets in the Holy Scriptures.

Word of Truth
James 1:18

He chose to give us birth through the word of truth, that we might be a kind of firstfruits of all he created.

Word of Christ
Colossians 3:16

Let the word of Christ dwell in you richly as you teach and admonish one another with all wisdom, and as you sing psalms, hymns and spiritual songs with gratitude in your hearts to God.

Book of the Law

Nehemiah 8:3

He read it aloud from daybreak till noon as he faced
the square before the Water Gate in the presence of
the men, women and others who could understand.
And all the people listened attentively to the Book of
the Law.

The Scroll

Psalm 40:7

Then I said, "Here I am, I have come — it is written
about me in the scroll."

1. Give You New Birth

James 1:18

He chose to give us birth through the word of truth, that we might be a kind of firstfruits of all he created.

1 Peter 1:23

For you have been born again, not of perishable seed, but of imperishable, through the living and enduring word of God.

2. Illuminate Your Mind With Understanding

Psalm 119:130

The unfolding of your words gives light; it gives understanding to the simple.

3. Revive Your Soul

Psalm 19:7

The law of the Lord is perfect, reviving the soul.

4. Sanctify You
(Make You Holy; Set You Apart for God)

John 17:17

Sanctify them by the truth; your word is truth.

1 Peter 1:2

Who have been chosen according to the foreknowledge

of God the Father, through the sanctifying work of the Spirit, for obedience to Jesus Christ and sprinkling by his blood: Grace and peace be yours in abundance.

5. Help You to Be Obedient

Psalm 119:34

Give me understanding, and I will keep your law and obey it with all my heart.

Romans 1:5

Through him and for his name's sake, we received grace and apostleship to call people from among all the Gentiles to the obedience that comes from faith.

6. Give You Faith

Romans 10:17

Consequently, faith comes from hearing the message, and the message is heard through the word of Christ.

Romans 12:3

For by the grace given me I say to every one of you: Do not think of yourself more highly than you ought, but rather think of yourself with sober judgment, in accordance with the measure of faith God has given you.

Ephesians 3:12

In him and through faith in him we may approach God with freedom and confidence.

7. Give You Hope

Romans 5:3–5

Not only so, but we also rejoice in our sufferings, because we know that suffering produces perseverance; perseverance, character; and character, hope. And hope does not disappoint us, because God has poured out his love into our hearts by the Holy Spirit, whom he has given us.

Romans 15:4

For everything that was written in the past was written to teach us, so that through endurance and the encouragement of the Scriptures we might have hope.

8. Make You Wise

Psalm 119:98

Your commands make me wiser than my enemies, for they are ever with me.

Proverbs 2:6

For the Lord gives wisdom, and from his mouth come knowledge and understanding.

James 1:5

If any of you lacks wisdom, he should ask God, who gives generously to all without finding fault, and it will be given to him.

9. Cleanse Your Heart

John 15:3

You are already clean because of the word I have spoken to you.

Hebrews 4:12

For the word of God is living and active. Sharper than any double-edged sword, it penetrates even to dividing soul and spirit, joints and marrow; it judges the thoughts and attitudes of the heart.

10. Give You Comfort

Psalm 23:4

Even though I walk through the valley of the shadow of death, I will fear no evil, for you are with me; your rod and your staff, they comfort me.

Psalm 119:50

My comfort in my suffering is this: Your promise preserves my life.

2 Corinthians 1:3–5

Praise be to the God and Father of our Lord Jesus Christ, the Father of compassion and the God of all comfort, who comforts us in all our troubles, so that we can comfort those in any trouble with the comfort we ourselves have received from God.

Chaplain (COL)
Scott McChrystal, USA (Ret)

Chaplain (Colonel) Scott McChrystal was commissioned in 1970 as a 2Lt in the infantry. He served 31 years on active duty, 10 as an infantry officer and the remainder as an Army chaplain. His line officer experience included a tour in Vietnam as an Infantry Platoon Leader and three assignments with the 82nd Airborne Division at Fort Bragg, North Carolina. As an Army chaplain, he had multiple tours at home and abroad. His final assignment was as the senior chaplain at the United States Military Academy at West Point, New York. He retired from active duty in 2005.

His decorations and awards include the Distinguished Service Award, the Bronze Star, the Combat Infantryman's Badge, the Master Parachutist Badge, and the Army Ranger Tab.

Chaplain McChrystal presently serves as the Military/VA Representative and Endorser within the Chaplaincy Department for The General Council of the Assemblies of God. Chaplain McChrystal and his wife, Judy, live in Springfield, Missouri, and have four children. ∎

On the left, 1Lt Scott McChrystal and his infantry platoon wait for helicopters that will insert them on a search and destroy mission to the west of Danang, South Vietnam, 1971. Above, Chaplain McChrystal prepares to deliver a public prayer at the United States Military Academy at West Point, New York, 2003.

Judy and I have been encouraged by the positive response to **Volume 1, Training for Spiritual Excellence**. Military men and women, both home and abroad, have reported that this book has helped them in the daily battles of life. Equally gratifying have been the enthusiastic responses by military family members and other civilians who have been using the book as well.

We trust that **Volume 2, Fortifying Your Spiritual Foundation**, is equally helpful. Regardless of age or maturity as a Christian, it's important to examine our spiritual foundation on a regular basis and make adjustments as needed. Weak or shaky spiritual foundations can be transformed into strong ones.

Volume 3: Building Resilient Marriages and Families is now available. Since 9/11, many servicemen and women and their families have been directly engaged in a war against terrorism. Tens of thousands of warriors have deployed multiple times with no end in sight. While family members may not enter the geographical zone of combat, they face equally tough battles on the home front.

So how do warriors and families maintain resiliency to keep going? We find our answer in God. He provides the spiritual weaponry and resources to prevail in any situation against any enemy. *Building Resilient Warriors and Families* will lay out the principles, tactics, weapons, and resources available to every warrior and family. The book will deal head-on with some of the toughest issues of our times:

- *Enhancing Marriage*
- *Improving Communication*
- *Managing Finances*
- *Encouraging Faith in the Family*
- *Handling Conflict*
- *Raising Children in Today's World*
- *Finding Balance*

Resiliency in today's world is not an option.

Fortunately, the Lord has a plentiful supply for those who earnestly seek after Him.

Additional copies of this volume,
as well as other volumes, are available at
Our Web site: www.dailystrengthforthebattle.com
By e-mail: dailystrengthforthebattle@gmail.com
By mail: Warrior Spirit Publications
P.O. Box 8125, Springfield, MO 65801

Notes

Notes

Daily Strength **for the** **Battle**